Semi-Detached Teachers

School Development and the Management of Change Series

Series Editors: Peter Holly and Geoff Southworth
Cambridge Institute of Education
Cambridge, CB2 2BX, UK

School Development and the Management of Change Series: 7

Semi-Detached Teachers: Building Support and Advisory Relationships in Classrooms

Colin Biott

 The Falmer Press

(A member of the Taylor & Francis Group)
London • New York • Philadelphia

UK	The Falmer Press, Rankine Road, Basingstoke, Hampshire RG24 0PR
USA	The Falmer Press, Taylor & Francis Inc., 1900 Frost Road, Suite 101, Bristol, PA 19007

First published 1991

British Library Cataloguing in Publication Data
Biott, Colin
Semi-detached teachers: building advisory and support
relationships in classrooms. — (School development and the
management of change series; 7)
1. Schools. Teachers. Cooperation with teachers
I. Title II. Series
371.14

ISBN 1-85000-442-0
ISBN 1-85000-443-9 pbk

Library of Congress Cataloging-in-Publication Data
Biott, Colin.
Semi-detached teachers: building advisory and support
relationships in classrooms / Colin Biott.
p. cm. — (School development and the management of
change series; 7)
Includes index.
ISBN 1-85000-442-0: — ISBN 1-85000-443-9 (pbk.):
1. Master teachers—Great Britain. 2. Group work in
education. 3. Teaching—Vocational guidance—Great
Britain. 4. School management and organization—Great
Britain. I. Title. II. Series.
LB2832.4.G7B56 1990
371.1′412—dc20

Typeset in 11/13 Garamond by
Chapterhouse, The Cloisters, Formby L37 3PX

*Printed in Great Britain by Burgess Science Press, Basingstoke
on paper which has a specified pH value on final paper
manufacture of not less than 7.5 and is therefore 'acid free'.*

Contents

Managing A Support Service

The School Context

Dedication

This book is dedicated to the hard-working advisory and support teachers
who gave time to talk with me.

Acknowledgments

I am grateful to the LEAs and schools which invited and allowed me to talk with the advisers, teachers and advisory teachers from whom I learned so much. In particular, it was the opportunities I had to take part in long evaluative conversations with advisory and support teachers which generated the momentum for me to try to understand better the nature of their complex and demanding role. The insights which form the basis of this book have been achieved through sustained professional collaboration.

I should also like to acknowledge the help of David Smith from the University of Sydney, Australia, who worked with me on an evaluation study whilst he was on study leave in the UK. His energy and vigour is a lasting inspiration.

I should especially like to thank Ian Heslop for the use of a personal evaluation statement.

List of Tables and Figures

Series Editors' Preface

In the not-too-distant future there could well develop a support vacuum within the educational system in the UK. Two related developments could contribute to the formation of such a vacuum. With the advent of the Local Management of Schools (LMS), schools may decide that, when it comes to ordering their financial priorities, they cannot afford to buy in support and advice.

Presumably, consultancy and advisory support services come a long way down the list of their priorities — especially when the raw materials of daily classroom life (books, paper, learning materials and equipment, etc) have to be obtained and budgeted for. And just when schools could be tempted to retrench and forego the assistance of external support agents, many of those support agents (e.g. members of the advisory teams in Local Education Authorities) are being encouraged to change their spots and become the guardians of the National Curriculum. Their new brief is monitoring and inspection — the *external* surveillance of quality control when it comes to the implementation of the National Curriculum *inside* the school.

So, at the same time as schools may be persuaded to jettison the use of support agents, such people (in the form of LEA Advisers) may no longer exist anyway — thus the support vacuum.

Yet the evidence — from both sides of the Atlantic — points to the need for ongoing, developmental, collaborative support in the effective mobilisation of school-improvement efforts. As this important volume amply demonstrates, in the 1980s we have not only registered this need for support, but also created a wealth of expertise and experience which could be tapped in the 1990s and beyond. On the one hand, 'minimalist' interpretations of school improvement do not include the support factor; on the other, minimalist approaches do not work.

Rather read this book, then, than make a cheap — but costly — mistake.

Hopefully, schools will realize that they cannot afford not to buy in support and advice and many of the semi-detached teachers about in this book will have taken the brave decision to 'hang on in there' — in support of real, lasting school improvement.

Peter Holly and Geoff Southworth
July 1990

Introduction

The main aim of this book is to enhance understanding of the role and work of advisory or support teachers: those semi-detached teachers who take the risk of doing their jobs in other people's schools and classrooms. A recent survey showed that there are more than four thousand such teachers in the UK. Most are experienced mid-career teachers who are currently on some kind of temporary secondment from classroom teaching. Studies of their work can help to explore issues about the occupational culture of teaching, teachers' careers, strategies for the professional development of teachers, curriculum and school development, and organizational change in LEAs and schools. The main challenge for many advisory teachers is to help teachers to learn from each other in the classroom at the very point where they interact with pupils or students. This is an enormous task given the nature of the teaching culture.

The first part of the book is focused on advisory teaching as a job. The opening chapter outlines the emergence of the role during the past decade as a result of a number of national projects and changing arrangements for the funding of the in-service education of teachers. The second chapter discusses how it feels to be an advisory teacher, with emphasis on the occupational culture of teaching and the sources of professional satisfaction and dissatisfaction. The third chapter then explores the extent to which advisory teaching may be a rewarding part of a teacher's overall career, and in what ways it may be appropriate to judge a period of semi-detachment as a rewarding phase in itself. It uses the concept of the lateral, individually-based career which does not necessarily imply vertical progression through an existing hierarchy of promotion points.

The second part contains two personal accounts by advisory teachers. In the first of these Mike Sullivan recalls what it was like for a seconded primary headteacher to subject himself to what felt like a 'long teaching practice'. He humorously describes the ironies of it all, but the reader will still be able to catch the sense in which it was a positive and valuable experience for himself and for the schools in which he worked. In Chapter 5, Graham Atkinson's self-critical review concentrates on his work with one teacher. From the basis of a recorded conversation, he reflects about the extent to which he may be developing cosy rather than critical partnerships and seeking to work with like-minded teachers instead of those who are resistant to change.

Part three concentrates on the implicit models of professional development which shape the practices of advisory teachers. In Chapters 6 and 7, Bridget Somekh and Patrick Easen advocate approaches which emphasize collaboration and enquiry. Somekh provides a rationale and some practical advice on the use of action research as a means for advisory teachers to support classteachers' professional development. Easen then gives a useful categorization of strategies for classroom-based work in order to point to the weaknesses of many of the common strategies in use. He argues that collaborative classroom control between the two teachers is the most effective arrangement for professional learning. It offers opportunities for the construction of shared meanings and understandings. Changes in the practice of teaching, he claims, require a transformation of meaning perspectives. That is because 'what teachers do about teaching is based on what they think about teaching'.

The fourth part of the book addresses issues in the management of support and advisory services. Both Maggie McKenna and George Robinson review how their own services have developed over time. McKenna shows how one LEA has reconceptualized the role of the visiting 'special educational needs' support teacher in mainstream schools. Her detailed account shows how pilot projects, enquiries, INSET and the use of external consultants have all helped both the support service and the schools to develop and clarify the roles, working principles and procedures of support. Like Somekh and Easen she emphasizes the value of action research as a key element. Robinson then recalls the difficulties of establishing a coherent and effective advisory teacher service during a time of expanding INSET provision, rapid national change and local upheaval. He traces the way in which the working conditions and practices of the service have been developed through a process of participative enquiry and policy making. The overall thrust is towards an entitlement model for the LEA, the schools and the advisory teachers themselves.

In the final chapter the focus shifts to the different school contexts in which the advisory teachers work. Using case-study material, it addresses the question of whether it is essential to have the right preconditions in the school before the support can be effective for the whole school, or whether advisory teaching projects can contribute towards the building of those conditions.

It is especially hoped that both experienced and new advisory teachers will find the book interesting and thought-provoking. One of the strengths of the job is that it has few routines and orthodoxies. It certainly doesn't seem to suit people who like to think that they know all the answers or those who like to be told what to do.

Being Semi-Detached

Chapter 1

Advisory Teaching:
An Uncertain Role in Transition

Colin Biott

The term 'semi-detached teacher' is used in this book to refer to those teachers, usually in mid-career and confident in their own professional practice, who have chosen to work in other people's classrooms and schools often for a specified period of secondment. The labels of advisory teacher, teacher-adviser and support teacher are those most commonly used to desribe this role. Other kinds of semi-detachment, such as that experienced in supply, temporary and part-time posts, or by peripatetic teachers who visit schools to teach invididual pupils will not be discussed here. The titles of support teacher and advisory teacher have been used interchangeably in some LEAs (local education authorities). In others they each have specific meanings such as when the former is used to describe a role which is focused on giving 'support' to children and the latter on giving 'advice' to teachers. In this book the labels are used interchangeably according to the label used in the LEA to which the extract refers. In any case, the discussions of modes of working often demonstrate that rigid boundary distinctions are inappropriate.

The role of the 'advisory' and 'support' teacher has developed in an ad hoc way in many of the local education authorities in the UK during the 1980s. Many of the jobs have been funded by national projects and programmes, such as Education Support Grants (ESG), the Technical Vocational Education Initiative (TVEI), and the TVEI Related In-service Training project known as TRIST. Others have been created since the introduction of the Local Authority Training Grant Scheme (LEATGS) in 1987, and many have developed as part of changing approaches in the provision of support for children with special educational needs in ordinary schools, particularly since the 1981 Education Act. The HMI report on the first year of LEATGS notes how an advisory teacher's function had been broadly defined 'to work alongside other teachers in respect of the development of a subject or an aspect of the curriculum and to be responsible to the adviser/inspector for that area of the curriculum' (DES, 1989b, para. 3.14).

The variety of posts and arrangements existing at that time is also described in the report:

> some were seconded for periods of one to three years; a few had permanent appointments or had been redeployed from some other role such as working in a remedial education unit; some had held posts as headteachers or deputies or had been heads of department; the majority had proven experience and expertise in a phase, subject or cross curricular area. Advisory teachers were employed on a variety of pay scales ranging from main professional grade to that of head of a group 5 school. For some the salary level caused difficulty in terms of status; important when holding discussions with headteachers. (DES, 1989b, para. 3.13)

Further evidence is provided in the Association for Science Education survey of 121 advisory teachers for Primary Science and Technology (Gaskill, 1989) which shows that of the ninety-eight with secondments, sixty-six had general LEA secondments whilst thirty-two were seconded to return to their original schools. The survey was used to paint a picture of the 'average' advisory teacher for primary science and technology as:

> a female junior school teacher who has contributed some fifteen years classroom service. When this teacher was given a three year ESG secondment in September 1986 there was an agreement that a post would be found within the LEA at the end of the secondment. There was a pay increase of some 9 per cent on taking up the post of advisory teacher as the job carried an incentive B allowance and the teacher had been on Main Scale.

According to the HMI report, the predominant areas of appointment in 1987 were for language, mathematics, science, information technology, special educational needs and multicultural education, whilst some LEAs also included early years, equal opportunities, modern langauges, drama and humanities. This is confirmed in the fuller list produced from the Association for Science Education survey in Autumn 1988 (Gaskill, 1989). This gives the description of the posts and the numbers of advisory teachers in specific areas of work in the forty-three LEAs which responded. In addition to the subject areas mentioned above, TVEI, drugs education and home/school links were also well represented.

The HMI report describes the advisory teachers as 'highly motivated, hard working and, in some cases, inspirational in their teaching and support of schools'. They were said to have the necessary tact, diplomacy and knowledge which the job requires, and to be well regarded by the schools. Nevertheless, that section of the report concludes that, 'the lack of training offered to advisory teachers, the problems over their career structure and a failure by too many LEAs to define their role and relationship with other groups in the support services require urgent attention' (DES, 1989b, para. 3.16).

An Uncertain Role

The literature on advisory and support teaching, which, at the present time, is mainly to be found in journals and in evaluation reports also reflects a concern to define and clarify the nature of the task.

One of the earliest references (Jane and Varlaam, 1981) is to the Inner London Education Authority's school-focused INSET scheme in which three 'curriculum support teams' of three seconded teachers worked under the direction of a district inspector to assist staff in primary schools to develop the curriculum. The teams worked in the schools for one term on an aspect of the curriculum negotiated in advance with the school staff. Jane and Varlaam report that in the first year of operation (1979) the scheme suffered from an 'unclear public image' — 'Curriculum development undertaken as a co-operative exploration exercise by the staff of a school, albeit with some help from a curriculum support team, was a novel idea, not easily understood by the host school' (p. 31).

Six years later in 1985, twelve LEAs began similar projects with funding from the Education Support Grant for 'Improving Urban Primary Schools'. Each of the projects had an 'enabling team' of support teachers, varying in size from one teacher in one LEA to seven teachers in another (DES, 1989a, p. 3). At the same time ESG projects were also being established in mathematics, and primary science and technology with advisory or support teachers as a central feature. Nevertheless, we find that new ESG advisory teachers for primary science still found, according to de Boo (1988), that there were 'few precedents' and even fewer 'records' to provide them with useful guidance about how to undertake the work. He noted how most support teachers in schools had, up to that time, concentrated on children with language or other learning difficulties, whereas his task was to 'change teachers' attitudes towards science and the practice of it in their classrooms'. He said that 'with just three years in which to do this, it felt like jumping into the deep-end knowing only that the water was not ice-cold' (p. 12).

As in the earlier ILEA project there was also still a problem of overcoming the doubts of the teachers in some schools which were scheduled to receive support. The HMI report on the ESG 'Improving Urban Primary Schools' project, for example, reminds us of how:

> Initially some heads and teachers were ambivalent about the contribution that enabling teams might make to their schools. They recognised the value of extra help in developing aspects of the practice to which they were committed but were concerned that selection to take part in the project singled them out as in some way failing or ineffectual. Thus they were somewhat apprehensive about the prospect of having the work of their pupils and methods of teaching placed under scrutiny. This meant that some enabling teams had particular difficulty in establishing effective relationships in some schools. (DES, 1989a, para. 15)

Returning to the role of the 'semi-detached teachers' themselves, Holly, James and Young (1987) also reported how the advisory teachers in the TRIST project lacked a suitable definition of their responsibilities and 'much had to be learned on the hoof!' Nevertheless, in spite of this lack of certainty about the role there was evidence that it was being seen as a key element of national and local strategies to promote and support school development. The TRIST evaluation, for example, referred to advisory teachers as 'the big success story', 'the leading lights' of having 'immense street credibility' and of being 'expensive but worth it' (Holly *et al.*, 1987). Partly as a result of this experience and that of the ESG scheme, the introduction of the LEA Training Grants Scheme (LEATGS) in April 1987 then gave another boost to the numbers of advisory teachers in post:

> Experience of advisory teachers under the Education Support Grant (ESG) scheme encouraged many LEAs to see them as a vital ingredient in their INSET arrangements. Hence there has been an increase in the number of advisory teachers employed by many LEAs, ranging from two to sixteen per LEA in the first year, with further appointments planned for 1988/89. (DES, 1989b, para. 3.9)

There was evidence, then, that advisory teachers were being recognized as 'a vital ingredient' in staff development strategies and they were being used to support the introduction of the national curriculum. A survey in 1990 indicated that there were some 4,500 advisory teachers nationally with an average of forty per LEA (Blanchard *et al.*, 1990).

A Role in Transition: The Case of Special Educational Needs

The lack of certainty about the role seems to derive less from doubts about its worth than from its transitional nature. Both the advisory teachers and the schools have been learning from trial and error. To some extent, the diversity and variation in practice is to be expected in view of the differences in projects and programmes and in the different arrangements across the LEAs. The variation in Special Educational Needs Support Services helps to illustrate the ways in which rapid changes of policy have lead to uneven developments and transitional problems of re-adjustment.

The 1986 NFER study of the support services for special educational needs in local authorities revealed considerable variation in the seventy-seven which responded to the survey (Hegarty, 1988; Moses, Hegarty and Jowett, 1988). Apart from the differences in title, size and organization, there were differences in the nature of the services. Some were solely or mainly advising teachers in the schools, whilst others taught the children directly. The former tend to have less staff overall, with a bigger proportion on higher salary grades. The rapid changes are reflected in the response of two-thirds of the authorities which had claimed, between 1981 and 1986, to have achieved major innovations in their support services. In that period, a fifth had combined separate forms of provision into a single generic service for all pupils with special needs and for their teachers in ordinary schools.

It is not surprising, then, that the HMI survey of ten LEA Support Services for Special Educational Needs, carried out between 1986 and 1988 (DES, 1989c), revealed that 'several services were struggling to establish their own code of practice in the absence of an LEA policy, and too many services were working in isolation from other parts of the LEA's advisory network' (para. 9). It is perhaps to be expected, therefore, 'that about one third of the services visited had not yet worked the "whole school approach" through insufficient practical detail to be able to effectively assist the schools to understand the concept and work towards its implementation' (para. 17).

In this volume Maggie McKenna (Chapter 8) takes up this issue and describes the way in which the support service in one LEA has attempted to build its 'whole school' approach systematically through collaborative professional development and action research for both the support team and for the schools. In Chapter 9, George Robinson traces some key issues in the management of the whole LEA service during a period of rapid change.

Tasks and Strategies

Turning from the management of whole services to the ways in which the

7

support teachers actually work, we find similar diversity and similar problems of role definition. Dyer (1988) has noted the change in title of the specialist journal from 'Remedial Education' to 'Support for Learning' and he traces the shift from the term 'remedial' which labelled the children themselves to the more active notion of giving support at the point where teaching and learning meet. He recognized, at the same time, the transitional nature of some of the practices he had observed. For this reason he included the category of 'remedial support' to denote an approach which combines the 'new' terminology with the 'old' arrangement of withdrawing children into a separate group. Dyer's classification of types of support is a useful step towards clarity. He has subdivided the three broad categories of

1   support for pupils;
2   support for teacher/pupils; and
3   support for curriculum and materials development

into more detailed applications:

1   *Direct pupil support (or one-to-one support)*
    (a)   In-class support   obviating problems as they arise in a lesson.
    (b)   Preparational support   to prepare the pupil for an ongoing lesson (e.g., teaching sight vocabulary of key words).
    (c)   Remedial support   pupils are withdrawn into a separate group for extra tuition (may have little impact on the whole-school approach).

2   *Teacher/pupil support*
    (a)   General class support   team teaching in which the teachers' roles are ideally not distinguished.
    (b)   Consultative support   to respond to immediate problems or to 'get ahead' of potential problems.
    (c)   Analytical support   to detect what might be going wrong in organization, preparation or in the learning process.
    (d)   Observational support   to observe a specific point in classroom organization, lesson

		preparation or the pupil's learning strategy (likely to follow (c) above).
(e)	Substitutional support	the support teacher takes over the teaching of a lesson.
(f)	Specific (in-class) support	the follow-up to the analysis of a difficulty (recommended only as a specific focus where direct pupil in-class support is already practised).
(g)	Specific withdrawal support	for a short time span as part of the general support strategy.

3 *Support in curriculum delivery*

(a)	Planning support	support in planning to identify potential pitfalls for pupils.
(b)	Material (preparation) support	help to make materials or make commonly used materials accessible to certain pupils.
(c)	Curriculum support	support to maintain the integrity of the curriculum for low attainers.

(after Dyer, 1988, pp. 7–10)

Dyer does observe that 'in any given situation several functions of support, which can be identified separately, may be happening simultaneously' (p. 8), and he points out how some of the categories are closely interrelated. Such a classification, then, contributes towards more precise and focused discussion about the work of support teachers. Dyer, himself, uses it to pose questions about which support is desirable at a particular time in a school's development, and which support is economically possible.

For the support or advisory teachers themselves, the range and balance of their tasks are related directly to issues of scale and scope. The proportions of time which may be spent on the different aspects of their work will depend upon the number of teachers and schools they are expected to support, and upon the degree of depth and quality they attempt to achieve. In a study of the work of thirty-three support teachers for a range of subject areas in one LEA, I found that the proportion of time which they spent in classrooms was a matter for contentious debate. Some of those managing the support teachers thought that they should aim to spend 80 per cent of the time working in classrooms, regardless of whether they were attempting to promote cross curricular themes or support single subject developments. On the other hand, whilst the support teachers saw classroom support as their central task they knew that there was a limit to the amount of time that they could spend engaged in work of worthwhile quality. According to their own judgments the lowest reported time spent in classrooms was 5 per cent and the highest was 80 per cent. Of those LEA support teachers who judged their actual time spent in classrooms to be the ideal amount, the range was from 15 per cent to 80 per cent of the week. Fourteen of the thirty-three would like to have been able to spend more time in classrooms, but the obligation to do other kinds of work made it untenable.

The most pressing problem was that of finding time to plan and review their work with teachers. This was partly a problem of lack of time, but as Sullivan reports in Chapter 4 'often classteachers would regard these preliminaries as a waste of time' in any case. In my own survey of 340 teachers who had worked with ESG support teachers for primary science in the one LEA, only eleven (3.2 per cent) said that they had spent a lot of time planning. Most (68.5 per cent) only met the support teacher for a brief chat in snatched time during breaks between lessons. As one support teacher said, 'We try to have ten minutes or so to evaluate at the end of a lesson, but there is pressure of time in class teachers to prepare the next lesson. It tends to be often done while we clear away.'

As will be discussed in the next chapter, the semi-detached teacher is also usually in a hurry, and is often dashing between schools, hurrying to finish a lesson or talking fast. When asked about the profile of their work, the following range of activities other than classroom support were mentioned. Table 1.1 indicates the difference between the numbers actually engaged in these activities and the numbers who would ideally spend some of their time on them.

To some extent, the diversity in the patterns of work of these advisory and support teachers was due to the variety of the themes, arrangements and conditions of their work. The factors included:

- secondments or permanent appointments
- varied duration of secondments
- secondments from the LEA or the school
- either attached to a national programme/project, an established LEA service or a recent local initiative
- varied locations and work bases
- either single subject or cross curricular themes
- direct or indirect attachment to LEA advisers with varied degrees of guidance

Table 1.1 Activities other than classroom support reported by Advisory Teachers

Activity	Number of times mentioned (n = 30)	
	Ideal	Actual
Preparing materials/resources	22	16
In school 'fixing' Talking to teachers Planning/review	18	14
Inset	18	15
Admin	14	16
Team building Team review/debrief Team maintenance	11	10
Meeting/committees	8	7
Writing reports etc.	6	5
Prof devp (self) Reading Thinking National liaison	6	7
Home visits	1	—

- different types of schools or range of schools (all secondary or all primary schools or cross age phases)
- dealing with different categories of staff
- different arrangements for gaining access to schools (included formal bids from schools for support, 'officially' targetted schools or 'cold calling')
- working as individuals or in teams of different sizes

On the other hand, Straker (1988) also found great diversity in the way in which ESG mathematics advisory teachers worked in five different LEAs. He saw both strengths and weaknesses in this diversity of roles. The weaknesses were that there were no guidelines, no firm evidence about what constitutes the most effect practices and therefore there were problems about the organization of effective INSET. The main strength, he claims, arises from the absence of an imposed national job description. It means that the advisory teachers are able to vary their work to respond to local needs.

Of all of these activities in which advisory teachers are involved, it is classroom support which seems to be most challenging. This is discussed more fully in the next chapter, and the accounts by Graham Atkinson

(Chapter 5) and Mike Sullivan (Chapter 4) give some insights into how it feels to work in other people's classrooms. As Holly *et al.* (1987) observed, about the TRIST advisory teachers, their 'status-free, non-hierarchical credibility provided them with a measure of role conflict and ambiguity'. In some cases the support teachers sensed a negative attitude towards themselves from classteachers, and in a few cases there was explicit hostility because of the threat of interference in their work. Where more friendly and encouraging relationships were established, questions of worthwhileness and benefit still applied. As noted in the HMI report on the Special Educational Needs Support Services, there were times when the two teachers in the classroom 'did not combine their efforts in a coherent manner' and sometimes the 'second teachers were observed spending considerable periods in inactivity while one teacher lectured to the class'. There is, then, more to being a support teacher than being a 'second red pen' or an 'extra pair of hands'.

Questions about the effectiveness of promoting change through classroom support hinge around the concept of professional development which underpins it. In this book both Bridget Somekh (Chapter 6) and Patrick Easen (Chapter 7) explore this point, arguing for what Easen calls the building of a 'respectful but enquiring relationship with the classteacher'. Both emphasize the importance of *collaboration* and *enquiry*, and of engagement with genuine issues. Easen bases his views of advisory and support teachers' strategies on the assumption that classroom practice can only be transformed when the teacher's meaning perspective itself is transformed. The isolationist and individualistic aspects of teaching have, however, tended to limit teachers' potential for learning from each other at the point where they interact with their learners. The classroom-based work of the semi-detached teachers does offer scope for professional learning of significance, but certain strategies may provide little more than help with immediate practical problems.

The Advisory Role and the School Context

The title of advisory or support teacher, then, has little significance, either nationally or locally, unless the person in that role is able to give appropriate, timely and meaningful advice or support to teachers in schools. The type of support which is given may range from practical and ephemeral help with an obvious and easily visible problem, to shared enquiry which discovers and addresses fundamental issues or dilemmas in teaching or learning. The latter is likely to have a more enduring influence upon the professional development of both partners, but it is also harder to achieve because it is more demanding and more threatening. The form of support achieved will depend to some extent upon the skills and dispositions of the supporter or adviser and the classteacher, but it will also depend upon the culture of the workplace.

Little (1988) has argued that the day-to-day organization of schools is not conducive to influencing teaching. She has conducted a series of four studies into various aspects of teacher leadership in schools in the USA, including the work of administrators, teachers, teacher-advisers and the California Mentor Teacher Program. She has noted that:

> Teachers placed in positions that bear the titles and resources of leadership display a caution towards their colleagues that is both poignant and eminently sensible. The relation with other teachers that is implied by terms like mentor, advisor, or specialist has little place in the ordinary workings of most schools. Even the simple etiquette of teacher leadership is unclear. (p. 84)

In assessing the prospects for teacher leadership in schools, she emphasizes the importance of gauging teachers' everyday responses to two possibilities: that of classroom observation and the acceptance of specially designated leaders. On the point of observation she says:

> the prospects for leadership can be judged in part by whether teachers have developed, or are prepared to develop, a close working knowledge of one another's teaching, based on observation and in-depth discussion. . . . A school's culture is conducive to leadership by teachers when teachers are in one another's classrooms for the purposes of seeing, learning from, commenting on, and planning for one another's work for students. (p. 87)

On the issue of the degree of acceptance of leadership she refers to the way in which specially designated teachers will attempt to influence the curriculum and the day-to-day classroom work of other teachers and then says that:

> A school's culture is conducive to leadership by teachers when such initiative is acceptable. To assess the prospects for leadership in a school, then, one might ask: 'What latitude will teachers accord a colleague who is clearly recognised as a "master teacher"?' (p. 88)

These issues about the occupational and organizational cultures of teaching will be discussed more fully from the view point of the advisory teachers in

Chapter 3 and in relation to school contexts in Chapter 10. At this point, however, it does seem important to signal that the future development of advisory and support teaching raises as many, if not more, questions about the organization and nature of the profession and schools as it does about the selection and training of individuals for the job.

The main theme of the book, then, is about building the conditions for both classteachers and semi-detached teachers to learn together. The next chapter addresses the issue of how it feels to be semi-detached: to lose some of the cover of the occupational culture of teaching.

Chapter 2

Being a Support or Advisory Teacher: Satisfactions and Dissatisfactions

Colin Biott

The purposes of this chapter are to explore how it feels and what it means, to be a support teacher. Some of the characteristics of the occupational culture of teaching suggest that a period of semi-detachment may be problematic. Firstly, there is the loss of control of time and space in the classroom which is the teacher's workplace. The classroom is, according to Alexander (1984), the 'creation of a world in his or her [the teacher's] own image . . . comprehensive and uninterrupted over time and space' (p. 165). Those who no longer have their own classrooms and have become 'semi-detached' have thus temporarily relinquished the independence and control which they have experienced in their former work. Defining control as 'the reduction of uncertainty' gives a clue to the significance of this occupational change.

As will be discussed later in this chapter, the job of advisory and support teaching brings with it an increase in the uncertainty and unpredictability which comes from working in other teachers' classrooms. There are some aspects of classroom life which have been socially and historically constructed over time and which will have a reassuring familiarity to all former pupils and especially to those who eventually become teachers themselves. This embedded nature of the pupil and teacher roles is partly what makes it possible for support teachers to work instantly in new settings with children whose names, personalities and learning styles they do not know. It is, perhaps, not so much a problem of unfamiliarity as of lack of authority and predominance which may make the support teacher feel strange in another teacher's classroom. The implications of this for the personal status of the support teacher will be discussed later. In what circumstances and in what ways might the support teacher feel like a visitor, a welcome guest, a colleague, a respected expert, a representative of 'the office' or a meddling nuisance? What are the symbols, set-pieces and rhetoric of temporarily entering a series of different and previously uninterrupted classrooms?

Secondly, it has been noted how teachers begin to attach importance to the 'psychic rewards' which come from the responses of the children they teach (Lortie, 1975). Children, in effect, become the teachers' 'reality definers' (Riseborogh, 1985). Nias (1989) has recently illustrated how the children play a part in shaping a primary schools teacher's self-image. As one of her interviewees said, 'Blow the others [teachers] — I keep going because the kids enjoy what I'm doing and that tells me I am right' (p. 55). Nias emphasizes the importance of the children as a reference group in making teachers feel either professionally competent or inadequate: 'All in all, their [children's] capacity to shape, confirm and destroy individuals' future careers, by moulding the latter's view of their own characteristics, capabilities and aspirations, has probably so far been underestimated' (pp. 55–6).

It is not surprising, then, that many support teachers continue to refer to the children's learning progress as their main concern even when they may see a large number of children, only infrequently and briefly, and sometimes only for a stint of less than half a term. Even though they were working simultaneously in many different schools and classrooms, many of those interviewed talked as though their main concern was that the children would benefit. Except for those whose role is to support the learning of specifically identified pupils over an extended timescale, such as special needs support teachers, it is likely that their direct impact on the children will be partial and marginal. What does remain possible for the itinerant support teacher, however, is the feedback which they get from children's immediate responses to them. This is why 'flying visits' to conduct impressive demonstration lessons can become seductive, especially for ex-secondary school teachers working as support teachers in primary schools where the children are reassuringly lively, malleable and animated.

What seems difficult for advisory and support teachers, especially in the early stages of their new posts, is for them to change their concept of 'their learners' from the children to the teachers with whom they work. The main implication of this change to 'teachers as learners' is that it is other teachers and not other children who then become the main validators of the support teachers' feelings of professional credibility. It is other teachers who influence their feelings of personal worth. As will be explored later, this can render the support teachers vulnerable to rejection and even humiliation by teachers who are hostile to the initiatives which they represent. This was apparent during the first year of some ESG projects which began in 1985–86 and which were affected to some extent by the teachers' pay dispute. How do the classteachers and the support teachers sustain their self-images in these circumstances?

This brings us to the third feature of the occupational culture of teaching which is helpful in understanding the significant nature of the change of role to semi-detached teacher. It concerns the way that teachers relate to other teachers in staffrooms. Pollard (1987) has called staffrooms the places where teachers can be 'temporarily insulated from the demands of the children in their classes. Staffrooms are thus one critical area in which confidences are exchanged, tension is released and in which staff cultures develop' (p. 104). The 'hallmark' of this culture is said to be 'practicality' and 'experience' and in this sense the staffroom culture may fail to reflect the primary school teachers' personal and professional commitment to teaching. According to Pollard, the staffroon talk revolves around 'topics which are "common denominators" and which strengthen the in-group feeling in the face of perceived external pressure and despite its own underlying tensions' (p. 105). The discourse of these common denominators is said to be insular and relatively static.

Following this analysis, and having in mind Hammersley's (1984) view of staffroom talk as preserving dignity and maintaining solidarity, it is not surprising that many advisory and support teachers have felt uncomfortable and awkward in the staffrooms of some of the schools in which they have worked. For instance, the team of support teachers in one project remembered its early days in the schools and one of them said:

> we were made to feel that the staffroom wasn't for us — I think that's always stuck — it's stuck with me very strongly. The other side of the coin was the way that they said that they expected us to go in there.

In another school:

> The head asked us to go in with the teachers — she allotted us to teachers to work with them on the first morning. The teacher I worked with was on playground duty and she was a bit concerned about what would happen about coffee money, and I ended up not going in the staffroom at all.

While the support teachers remained wary all through the two and a half year project, about their place in the staffrooms, it was at the beginning that the school staff clearly communicated their collective resentment at the intrusion of what support teachers represented. On one occasion a member of the team wanted to talk to one of the staff at breaktime and was kept at the door during the conversation. Such incidents were related and discussed and they rapidly became part of the project team's shared history as its members developed a heightened awareness of feelings of belonging and marginality.

Much of this was focused on its experience of relating to the staff as a whole. The support teachers became keen observers of staffroom relationships and politics. Towards the end of the project, when they had built positive working relationships with some individual teachers, they still retained strong reservations about their place in the staffroom. As one support teacher said to another:

> Remember — I said — she was a lovely person to work with in the classroom, but she ignored me in the staffroom. I stopped trying to talk to her in there.

It was felt that the enthusiasm and commitment which the classteacher and support teacher were able to share in the privacy of the classroom were to be kept separate from staffroom talk. There grew an implicit understanding that an individual teacher's involvement with the project team in her own classroom was not incompatible with her demonstration of solidarity with the collective staff resentment and resistance to the intrusion of imposed, external support teachers.

This kind of apparent discrepancy in interpersonal relationships is seen by Pollard to be of great significance as it points to the way in which teachers in schools need each other, but do not necessarily share fundamental values or perspectives: hence the need for the safe talk or the 'common denominators'. Eraut (1984) has referred to this as the language of 'talk about teaching' or the 'rhetoric of justification' which has been developed carefully to preserve autonomy and justify habitual actions. The avoidance of topics of controversy or conflict can mean, as Easen (1985) observes, that 'instead of looking hard at any inadequacies in our ways of making sense of the world we become ever more defensive of them' (p. 18). Nias (1987) attributes this reluctance of teachers to engage in genuine exchange of views on educational issues partly to the results of their training which has been underpinned by the naturalism and pragmatism of Froebel and Dewey, and partly to features of their occupational lives in which they are short of time, and in which they belong to reference groups which protect them from challenge.

All of this adds up to considerable difficulties for the support teacher who is employed, as in the ESG projects, to effect the kind of changes in the schools which demand extensive discussion of fundamental issues. In the ESG Improving Urban Primary Schools Project, for example, one of the aims was to 'raise pupil performance by raising teacher expectations and improving their school's organisation, curriculum, arrangements for parental involvement and other policies' (DES, Circular 6184), and in the Primary Science and Technology Project, the support teachers were expected 'to work alongside teachers in classroom situations to assist and advise during the development of new courses or new methods of teaching practice' (local advertisement for a scale 3 support teacher).

Despite such explicit and public aims, the support teachers were often easily diverted, especially in the early stages, from discussing fundamental issues and principles to more limited but less threatening activities such as practical demonstrations and resource provision. This will be discussed more fully in a later section.

As well as the problems associated with staffroom talk there is what Gronn (1983) has called teachers' capacity to control the use of talk:

> teachers often carry the classroom superordinancy over into their relationships with their administrative superiors. They try to use words to get them to do things, just as they have learned to do with children. (p. 18)

One consequence, which Gronn explores, is the effect of this on the way in which principals in the USA or headteachers in the UK have 'to adjust to having teachers attempt to control them'. This he argues, 'means listening to staff speaking as authorities before replying authoritatively'. This has implications for the interactions between classteachers and support teachers in the sense that it will be the talk which does most of the work and which structures their relationships. The way in which this happens will vary with the settings in which the work is done. As yet little is known about how teachers and support teachers use talk to form the inter-subjectivity of their roles and so to make sense and meaning of their work together. Glib statements about 'negotiating' may conceal more than they reveal. It is sometimes apparent that 'negotiated' agreements in different schools and with a range of different teachers have a striking similarity to each other. This may be less a case of individual weaknesses in the practice of conversing, supporting or advising as of the way in which the interaciton has been socially constructed and the way in which it is shaped by the deeply embedded socio-political history of the everyday world of schools and the roles of those who visit them to offer support. For instance, there is evidence from the interviews that the new job of advisory or support teaching was often being defined in terms of 'what a good headteacher used to have time to do' or 'what an adviser would really like to do if it wasn't for all of the other things that have to be done'.

Much of what advisory teachers have been attempting to do has been aimed at affecting 'whole schools'. They have been attempting the kind of developments which require the staff to work together. However, the advisory teachers are not in a position to initiate cooperative or collegial staff activity where this does not already exist. Hargreaves (1982) has said that secondary school teachers, for instance, 'can co-ordinate with one another, certainly, but in matters of collaboration, the strong form of co-operation, they must be judged remedial'. He has noted how teachers are 'deeply involved with a culture of individualism' (p. 87). His interest in trying to 'rescue dignity from individual connotations' (p. 100) is echoed by Richards' (1987) concern to emphasize collaborative rather than individualistic approaches to primary teachers' work. He has said that:

> it is no longer reasonable to expect class teachers to cope individually and unaided with the range of demands now being made on them, and that individual self-sufficiency is undesirable in any case in view of the importance of continuity of experience and reasonable consistency of approach from class to class within the same school. (p. 194)

The development of what Campbell (1985) has called 'collegiality' and what Nias *et al.* (1989) have termed 'a culture of collaboration' is a matter for schools and not for the advisory or support teachers. On the other hand, they may provide experience of partnership which will help some teachers to recognize its value and change their orientation towards it. In this sense, the influence of advisory and support teachers, like the school-based training days, may be facilitating a move towards increased collaborative work in the schools. However, the support teachers will often be working in a range of different schools with varied degrees of collegiality and collaboration. Some schools are better prepared than others to make timely and appropriate use of external support and, as will be explored in the next section, and more extensively in Chapter 10, the school contexts do make a difference to the support teachers' feelings of satisfaction and dissatisfaction in their work.

Satisfactions and Dissatisfactions

What is Satisfying and Dissatisfying about the Job of Advisory Teaching?

Those readers with personal experience of different contexts will be able to set these ideas against their own observations and it is not claimed that the categorization offered here is either exclusive or generalizable. It derives from interviews with thirty-three support teachers and regular discussions with two ESG teams and a TVEI team over an extended period of time.

These ideas were validated by the support teachers themselves during the process of each study.

Nias (1989) has already suggested that the topic of teachers' job satisfaction lacks clarity of definition. She has based her own extensive analysis on an adaptation of the 'two-factor' hypothesis of Herzberg (1966) who treated job satisfaction and dissatisfaction separately and who had found, in a study of engineers and accountants, that the 'satisfiers' were intrinsic to the nature of the job itself and that the 'dissatisfiers' tended to derive from the context in which the work was done. Thus the removal of a dissatisfier would not guarantee an increase in satisfaction, as the two factors are not seen as interdependent aspects of motivation. As will be shown here, Nias found this to be an oversimplification in relation to the job of teaching.

In her analysis, Nias (1989) differentiates between primary school-teachers in early and mid-career. As most support teachers may be said to be in mid-career it is interesting to consider the sources of 'mid-career' satisfaction and dissatisfaction that they may have been feeling in their work prior to taking up the new post and then to compare them with the factors affecting their feelings in their 'new' semi-detached role. The connections being made here are tentative and as yet there is insufficient evidence to draw firm conclusions.

Job Satisfaction

Nias found that the main 'satisfiers' in the second decade of teaching were:

Self-Esteem – the sense in which the job fits and feels right
Affective Rewards – feeling needed and valued, especially by the children
A Sense of Competence – knowing that they are good at their job
Working with Colleagues – broadening out from the classroom, and influencing and relating to adults
Personal Extension – seeking elements of variety and challenge
Intellectual Satisfaction – usually from activities outside of the classroom
Control and Freedom – usually in one's own classroom

The factors in this list which are most obviously reduced after a move to supporting teaching are those associated with the loss of 'control and freedom' which come from not having a classroom of their own, and the loss of 'affective rewards' from not having a continuous relationship with a group of children. On taking up the new post it is also evident that some support teachers feel a reduction in 'sense of competence' and of 'self-esteem' that comes from doubts about whether they will fit the new job. On the other hand, the job of support teaching may bring increased opportunities for **'personal extension'** and **'intellectual satisfaction'**, and, given a cohesive team of fellow support teachers, it will offer a strong sense of **'colleagueship'**.

The evidence from advisory teachers themselves, shows the importance of the satisfaction which derives from talking and working with other adults. During the final term of a two and a half year secondment the following sources of satisfaction were cited by a team of three ESG support teachers who had worked intensively in three schools. The list derived from discussions, was written by the author and was then edited by the support teachers:

1 Having the opportunity to observe and learn from teachers whose practice they admired, especially when there was also time to review and discuss progress in children's learning.
2 Working with a teacher without specifying separate functions in the classroom so that the partnership became genuinely collaborative.
3 Being involved in the planning, with teachers, of activities such as INSET which would involve the whole staff.
4 Having the opportunity to talk with headteachers to review their own work and devise strategies for the next stages of the project, especially when this was related to ways in which the project might help to initiate and sustain corporate change.
5 Being able to talk about philosophy and practice with an LEA adviser, especially related to ideas about the project's potential for influencing collective professional-development and curriculum change.
6 Learning from discussions within the team itself, especially being able to share enthusiasms, talk about anxieties and develop a sense of colleagueship.
7 Discussing evaluation papers and ideas about the project's development with the evaluator, and thus making critical sense of their roles and the nature of their task.

The list forms a retrospective view of what they had learned and gained from the job through working with other adults, and especially from a sense of colleagueship with headteachers and LEA advisers. This will be discussed further in the next chapter on career issues. This matches Nias's findings that for many teachers it was their work outside of the classroom which kept them mentally on their toes, and that most mid-career teachers had learned how to find intellectual stimulation through undertaking work out of school, with an increased number enrolling on advanced in-service courses.

Turning to their reasons for applying for the posts of support teacher, most of those in the whole LEA study said that they wanted to 'broaden their experience', 'have a change', 'meet a new challenge' or 'escape from the frustrations of a limiting job'. Other reasons were that it may lead to promotion or career development, that it was based upon a sense of competence and expertise and a will to contribute to the development of their subject or field. A further reason for some was the wish to work in a team, or to join a specific LEA adviser who was referred to as a mentor.

Expectations about the nature of the job revealed that many had associated the job with increased autonomy, more time, more freedom, more flexibility and extra responsibility. Other expectations related to their anticipation of the tasks to be undertaken: supporting curriculum initiatives, providing INSET, working with teachers and children in classrooms, making resources, giving advice and encouraging teachers to change.

Job Dissatisfaction

When analyzing the sources of teachers' dissatisfaction Nias (1989) found, unlike Herzberg, that it 'was virtually impossible to distinguish between the job itself and the context in which it takes place' (p. 103). She introduced the concept of 'non-satisfiers', to include the aspects of work which regularly cause unhappiness or frustration, as well as the 'dissatisfiers' which are more obviously contextual. The following non-satisfiers were found in the first and second decades of teaching:

First Decade	*Second Decade*
Administration and Communication	Stress and fatigue
	Conflict with other lives
Lack of coherence	Conditions within the schools
Lack of direction	Conflict with individual
Conflict with individual principles	principles
	Lack of influence
Lack of influence	Lack of autonomy
Stress and fatigue	

The 'dissatisfiers' were:

First Decade	*Second Decade*
Socially uncongenial schools	Insufficient resources
Work conditions	Public image of teaching
Lack of career prospects	
Career concerns	

(After Nias, 1989. pp. 105–30)

Turning to the support teachers and comparing their declared sources of dissatisfaction with Nias's teachers we find that like teachers in their first decade of teaching, they also emphasized lack of coherence, lack of direction and problems with communication and administration. They made references to uncongenial aspects of their workplaces. When referring to the schools in which they worked, they said that they were unhappy when they felt that schools were unaware of how to use them, had conflicting expectations of them or even had negative attitudes towards them. When speaking of the general work context in the LEA they mentioned unclear expectations, unclear job specifications, lack of organization and communication, too many rules and too much 'red tape'.

An aspect of their dissatisfaction which matched that of 'second-decade teachers', also related directly to the thwarting of their expectations about the job, and their reasons for applying for the post. They found that contrary to expectations the job did not always offer more autonomy, more time, more flexibility and more freedom. In addition to the comments about rules and red tape they said that they sometimes felt that they lacked time, were spread too thinly, were not always trusted and sometimes they felt manipulated. The team of support teachers which was at the end of its secondment had found its lack of control of the pace of its work to be most disconcerting. It had usually been involved in too many concurrent and unconnected tasks, thus leaving insufficient time to plan and review. It recognized at the same time that this had been exacerbated, especially in the early stages of the project, by the team's own sense of urgency, of wanting to work with as many teachers as possible as soon as possible, in order to establish its presence and gain credibility for being hardworking.

Even though they were working hard for long hours none of the support teachers mentioned 'stress and fatigue', or 'conflict with other lives' as causing dissatisfaction when asked directly about it. They seemed to accept it as part of a new and challenging job which they had undertaken for a specified period. It would, of course, be naive to assume that they did not complain to each other at times about how overworked they were.

Like teachers in Nias's study the support teachers were very much concerned about their 'public image'. They felt at times that they were generally held in low esteem by schools, individual teachers and LEA advisers. This was apparent, for instance, in their uncertainty of how they were being judged, especially by those with whom they were not working directly. The recent rise in the number and visibility of support teachers in the LEA centre was increasing the demand to introduce guidelines from those who did not have detailed knowledge of their patterns of work. In particular, they were uneasy about the implicit judgments and also some explicit comments about how they should be spending their time. Whilst they themselves saw their classroom work as a very important aspect of their job, there was general agreement that unrealistic expectations were being held about the amount of time in which it was possible for them to engage in work of significance in classrooms. At the same time, it was thought that three things were being underestimated: the time needed to develop their own teamwork; the setting aside of time for planning and reviewing with teachers, and; space for their own professional development. These issues seemed to strike at their sense of autonomy and responsibility and at their feelings of being trusted. It highlighted the uncertain 'public image' of support teaching. Those who had previously been in senior posts in schools were tending to sense this apparent reduction in professional standing most acutely. These feelings also tended to vary according to the team, project or adviser to whom the support teachers were attached. The uneven nature of the various arrangements for providing sustenance for the support teachers themselves was a cause of some tensions. Ironically, the stronger that some teams became, the more that some of the other support teachers reported feeling excluded and isolated.

To some extent the 'public image' of the support teachers was seen to be dependent on the advocacy of the LEA advisory service. It was felt that feedback about support teachers' work is given to advisers both formally from headteachers and teachers and also informally through existing networks and the 'LEA grapevine'. Dissatisfaction arose where the support teachers sensed that a general, negative image of their role was being created through ad hoc judgments about their work. In contrast, morale was raised when it was found that some advisers had been helping to enhance the general reputation of the support teacher role through their informal talk in the LEA.

The dissatisfaction which arose from 'conflict with individual principles' during first decade in teaching was also evident in the support teacher's comments at the end of their secondments. They felt that some of their deeply held commitments and principles had been compromised or suspended during their work with some teachers. The avoidance of possible rejection by teachers had, at times, weakened their resolve or diluted the criteria they would use to judge their own practice.

The feeling of having a 'lack of influence' was also apparent in the comments of the team towards the end of its project. Dissatisfaction arose from the thought that their work may have no lasting impact on the schools or the teachers. They had been disappointed to find that some teachers had regarded the new classroom strategies as feasible only when two teachers were present. Some of their work may have been merely a response to immediate or transient needs. They described 'one-off' demonstration lessons and accompanying classes on visits out of school with no follow-up, as examples of the kind of fruitless activity which they had undertaken. Unlike Nias's 'second-decade teachers', the support teachers did not mention issues related to 'lack of personal extension' when asked directly about sources of dissatisfaction. As indicated earlier, however, they were concerned about their future careers and this made them alert to any lack of opportunities for the kinds of personal extension which would enhance their own professional development. This is taken up in more detail in the next chapter.

Chapter 3

Advisory Teaching as a Rewarding Career Phase

Colin Biott

With no career structure for advisory teachers a minority of LEAs reported difficulty recruiting them. (DES, 1989b, para. 13)

The HMI report on the first year of the LEA Training Grant Scheme (DES, 1989b) suggests that problems over the career structure of advisory teachers require 'urgent attention', and it indicates that this may already be causing some difficulties in recruitment. Petrie (1988), writing from the perspective of a member of the ESG Primary Science and Technology Evaluation Project, also takes up this point. He believes that as a responsible employer an LEA should 'consider the options for the future and facilitate career progression as far as possible', and he goes on to say that 'a period of service as an advisory teacher can be an attractive option for the primary teacher seeking advancement'. This concept of career advancement seems to suggest vertical or hierarchical mobility. McLaughlin and Yee (1988) have called this an 'institutional view' of a career with its emphasis on organizational structures and extrinsic rewards. They have also described an alternative view of career as 'individually based' with an 'internally defined sense of advancement and satisfaction'. In their study of eighty-five teachers in California it was the latter, subjective conception of a satisfying career which was more important, with most of the teachers being 'interested neither in moving vertically into quasi-administrative or expanded teaching functions nor horizontally into administrative or central office resource positions' (p. 24).

The intention in this chapter is to consider support or advisory teaching as a temporary phase in a teacher's whole career. Firstly, it will be discussed as part of a hierarchically structured career which is based on the idea of upward steps and, secondly, as part of a career which is subjectively built according to an individual's sense of personal growth and reward.

Institutional Careers

I hear that you are getting a proper job now!

It was apparent during the interviews with support teachers and LEA advisers that some potential applicants were being dissuaded from applying for advisory and support teacher posts because it was being seen as an uncertain career step. For instance, one person, who had been interviewed for primary school deputy-headteacher posts prior to becoming an advisory teacher, had found that he was not getting onto the shortlists for interviews after having spent two years in advisory teaching. Such news spread quickly and it tended to lower the morale of the whole service. As well as the problems of uncertainty about the future positions achieved by advisory teachers after their secondments, there was a concern that job descriptions may not yet be specific enough to attract some ambitious candidates.

At the same time some of the LEA advisers thought that the job should not be seen as a standard route to a permanent post in the advisory service, which would imply that advisory teachers were junior or apprentice LEA advisers. It was suggested that support or advisory teachers' credibility with classteachers would begin to suffer if the job was seen as a means of permanent 'escape' from the classroom. It was thought, nevertheless, that after an immediate return to the classroom, many would subsequently become successful applicants for senior positions in schools or for LEA adviser posts.

Other general issues which relate directly to the concept of the 'institutional' career are the length of the secondments and the types of post. For example, there was some evidence that single-subject advisory posts were making some ex-primary school teachers concerned about their ability to keep up to date in other subject areas in the primary curriculum. It was thought that secondment periods for such posts should not be longer than for three years if those involved were intending to return to schools. This issue has become even more acute since the introduction of the Local Management of Schools (LMS), affecting both the recruitment and the arrangements for employment (see Robinson, Chapter 9 in this volume).

The whole LEA study revealed diversity and variation in the previous roles, current appointments and the pattern of secondments of the advisory and support teachers. A questionnaire was completed of thirty support teachers representing primary, secondary, subject-based, cross-curricular and special needs areas of work. These included people employed to promote both national and local initiatives. Four of the thirty had permanent support teacher appointments, each of them in the field of special educational needs. Of the remaining twenty-six, the length of secondments varied between one and five years. Eighteen of the thirty had been appointed within the year of study (1987–88) and twelve of those had been seconded for one or two years. Twenty of the thirty teachers had been working in secondary schools prior to their appointment, only two had come directly from primary school teaching, and the others had been involved in some aspect of special needs education across the LEA or in special schools. The secondary and primary school teachers had all held some form of coordinating role in their schools before the appointment. Twenty-one had taught for more than ten years and six of these had been teaching for over twenty years. None of those appointed had been teaching for less than six years.

Such a recent and rapid increase in numbers and the wide range and diversity of arrangements and personal characteristics make it difficult to manage the career interest of a support service as a whole unit. Furthermore, the constant turnover and consequent problems of establishing continuity make it difficult for an LEA to define the role of the service in relation to other aspects of the educational service into which ex-advisory teachers may move. For these reasons the 'institutional career' development of advisory and support teachers is probably best served through individual counselling and stewardship. This stewardship can begin prior to the appointment, with the teacher, headteacher and appropriate LEA adviser clarifying the way in which the period of secondment fits into the person's view of his or her longer term working life. Those teachers whose sights are fixed firmly on a 'mainstream' career through the school hierarchy, may need a different kind of post with different opportunities for professional learning when compared with a teacher who does not seek hierarchical advancement but who would like to spend some time in a different role for personal and professional extension.

Even when taking an 'institutional career' perspective, it is misleading to imply that advisory teachers and support teachers all share a common orientation to the job or that their long-term career aspirations are fixed prior to appointment. Evidence from studying the work of a small team of three ESG support teachers on an Urban Primary Project has shown how their varied reactions to similar opportunities for professional learning may be related to the way in which they begin to see their own futures. To some extent their views of the future are shaped by the new challenges and experiences of the job itself. One member of the team became overtly pragmatic towards the end of the project, and in discussions about the project's progress spoke consciously and explicitly with 'the voice of a classteacher'. That team member wished to return to class teaching:

> I would like the opportunity to make the developments I've been involved in with staff part of my own teaching repertoire. Many of the initiatives which have started were not part of my practice prior to the project.

That person was seeking 'consolidation' and a deeper sense of 'personal credibility' as a classteacher. During the project most of that member's own learning was said to have come from the classteachers in one of the schools where there was a feeling of 'fitting in to the school culture'.

In contrast, another team member claimed to have learned most from conversations with an LEA adviser and with one of the headteachers. That person was aware of developing a 'wider perspective':

> I'd like to work with teachers in a broader sense of the word right through an authority — looking at practice in general, maybe taking one or two aspects of it and developing it. Using skills I've learned in the project — how to cope with people. Maybe I'm prepared to stand back a little bit more now and not want to do everything at once as I did before. Also, I'm not as worried about being asked questions that would put me on the spot. I used to be worried about that in the early days — 'What if I'm asked a question and I don't know the answer?' It doesn't worry me in the least now. I don't tend to run around after people as much as I used to.

That team member was becoming more interested in working with a range of adults:

> I'd do it again, even starting under the same circumstances, provided I had the same support myself. It tests you. You get more thick skinned, working with different people with different attitudes to children and towards practice. You have to work in a way that they find comfortable, and then influence and offer support. You see things you don't like, but you have to block them out. I've learned a lot of skills.

The support teachers who participated in the whole LEA study were also mainly interested in a future role which maintained their involvement with adults whether or not it was in school. When asked directly about their future they mentioned: permanent support teacher or leader of a team of support teachers; having a coordinating role in schools; working in teacher education; 'any liaison or collaborative job'; 'something different in the adult world'; or 'an LEA adviser'. None of the thirty who completed written statements mentioned being a headteacher, but two said that they definitely did not wish to apply for that post. Some were entertaining ideas of leaving education for the 'world outside'. Eleven of the thirty felt sure that they would find it difficult to return to working in one school, and only four of the thirty felt that a return to work in one school would be a smooth transition. The reasons given were that it would probably lead to a feeling of 'being limited or trapped', it would involve being with 'cynical, unmotivated colleagues', or that it would require a return to 'too much conformity and a lack of risk taking'. The factors cited which would ease their return to school were all related to opportunities to use their new skills of working to influence adults. This would require what they judged to be the 'right environment': a 'school with an interest in enquiry', 'a collaborative school'.

Individually-Based Careers

The individually-based career may or may not involve a sense of vertical mobility. In the study mentioned earlier, for instance, McLaughlin and Yee (1988) found amongst Californian teachers that, 'even though some teachers wanted expanded or new roles, a vertical job structure did not fit their vision of career advancement' (p. 25).

The personal, internal view of career emphasizes the subjective meanings which occupational experiences have for the teachers. A satisfying, rewarding career is achieved when the professional opportunities and experiences fulfil needs for personal satisfactions (Bicklen, 1986) and 'psychic rewards' (Lortie, 1975). Like Bicklen, Nias (1989) has referred to the way in which women teachers may have been more able to redefine the meaning of career in this way and to turn their energy to a form of 'lateral extension'. Nias has suggested that it may be right to

> highlight the advantages to be gained from a flexible definition of 'careers' and to urge that these benefits be available to main bread-winners (usually men) whose morale and enthusiasm might also be revived by the opportunity sometimes to move sideways (or out) as well as up. (p. 76)

The question arising from this view of career is whether or not a stint of semi-detachment provides a sustaining or reviving occupational experience for teachers. McLaughlin and Yee cite two 'position-related factors' as critical to an individual's sense of professional growth: 'level of opportunity and level of capacity' (p. 26). Personal, professional growth varies according to the 'opportunity' and the 'capacity' characteristics of institutional settings.

The feeling of 'opportunity', of being able to 'improve performance, particularly in the context of collegial interaction' generates the enthusiasm and motivation to do even better. On the other hand, teachers with low levels of opportunity 'become burned out, just make it through the day, and trade on old skills and routines. They wind up in deadend jobs, going nowhere in terms of their career' (p. 28).

The concept of 'level of capacity' refers to the extent to which teachers feel able to shape and influence the goals and direction of their work and their institutions. This, according to McLaughlin and Yee, requires that the teachers have the necessary resources and the ability to use them. This feeling of 'capacity' is said to lead to a commitment to the organization and to the person's own career. A lack of capacity in this sense can lead to teachers 'lowering their aspirations, disengaging from the setting, and framing their goals only in terms of getting through the day. Teaching is thus apt to become just a job, not a career' (p. 29).

For McLaughlin and Yee, then, the concept of career as distinguished from a 'job' is one of 'a dynamic, developmental process that is constructed from features of the work environment — level of opportunity and level of capacity'. As such, it is best served by offering 'opportunities for lateral and temporary moves as well as for continuous stimulation and development' and not by the introduction of a generalized promotion system. This suggests that in order to understand teachers' subjective careers it is necessary to find out the extent to which their current work satisfies their individual needs. This view of 'career' focuses on the interrelationship between the personal and the professional lives of the teachers, and between individuals and their current work environment. McLaughlin and Yee approach this issue by considering the kinds of school environments that support a 'career'. An alternative starting point would be to identify the concerns and needs of the teachers themselves before making connections with their work environments.

Fuller (1969) has observed that teachers' concerns change and develop over time. She refers to three stages of concern: survival needs, task mastery and impact concerns. The idea of teachers moving through stages in this way helps to focus attention on their changing interpretations of occupational settings rather than simply on fixed responses to changing work contexts. Nias's (1989) use of Fuller's model to structure her recent account of UK primary schoolteachers' career development again provides a useful framework in which to explore the function of a period of semi-detachment as part of an individually-based career. It helps in the asking of questions about why some teachers may have chosen to change their work context. It also provides clues to understanding the characteristics of temporary semi-detachment as a phenomenon in its own right.

Semi-Detachment as a Career Phase

The support teachers in the whole LEA study had mainly been teaching between six and twenty years. It is likely that they had moved beyond *survival* in their previous posts in that they now felt able to meet the perceived requirements of their work. It also seemed that the schools in which some of them previously taught had been failing to nourish their individual career needs in the sense suggested by McLaughlin and Yee above. Eleven of the thirty teachers included negative reasons for escaping from the frustrations of a limiting job when explaining why they had applied for the support teacher posts.

Nias includes a period of *identification* as a teacher within the survival period to indicate the way in which significance was being given to the evaluative responses of colleagues and children, and showing how teachers' growing confidence depended to some extent on the feeling of referential support from those with whom they were working. Denscombe (1983) has emphasized the importance of membership of the culture of a specific school in what he has referred to as 'competent membership'. This implies that the teacher has learned, in that specific school, to share the values and ways of understanding and acting with other members. Because teachers change schools it is unwise to associate the need for identification or 'competent membership' with a specific point in an overall career. Indeed, as will be discussed later, the semi-detached role brings a new set of survival and identification problems.

The second phase, referred to as *task concerns*, includes a period of consolidation and of extension. The quest for personal extension which Nias's teachers spoke about, gives a clue to why some teachers may leave a permanent post in a school to take a temporary post as an advisory or support teacher. She describes teachers' desires for more responsibilities out of their classrooms, and for more intellectual challenges. For many, the latter was sought 'through intellectually-oriented reference groups, usually outside school'. This is echoed in interviews with the support teachers. They said that they sought to establish 'professional relationships which generate learning and energy for all concerned', 'to broaden experience' and to 'meet new challenges'. They were trying to create what Nias refers to as new ecologies in which to continue to grow professionally.

The third stage of career, according to Fuller, is that in which teachers have a concern for the degree of *impact* of their work. Nias refers to the way in which teachers wish to have a lasting impact upon the children and also seek to influence other people. As might be expected, the desire to influence other teachers is a strong motive of advisory and support teachers. Many expressed a commitment to particular theories and practices and welcomed an explicit brief to promote and support their development through initiatives such as TVEI and ESG projects. The temporary period of semi-detachment was, in these cases, offering sufficient difference to be refreshing. At the same time, it was also related directly to the previous post and it held some promise or expectation that it would enhance the next. In this sense it was helping some teachers to overcome one of the weaknesses of teaching as a lifetime occupation, which, as Nias notes, does not allow anyone 'to opt in and out at different points, in accordance with the dictates of felt-needs for personal growth or refreshment' (p. 75).

According to the 'institutional' view of career the main criterion of reward can only be applied post-hoc through the judgment of the value or status of the next or subsequent posts when measured against that which the teacher held immediately prior to taking up the support teacher appointment. It is this view which prompts Petrie (1988) to say that 'it would be a pity to return individuals to the classroom'. He makes a case for advisory teachers to be considered for the posts of LEA adviser, headteacher, teacher-educator and for positions in administration. Two LEAs, he notes, have already made known their intention to make 'supply headships possible for advisory teachers as a first step on that ladder' (p. 5). His own studies have indicated a 60 per cent overlap between the role of headteacher and advisory teacher. This kind of view of professional growth places value on experience and on skill acquisition and development. It suggests that, as the role of advisory teacher becomes more firmly established, it may be possible to modify and adapt job descriptions to meet the specific learning needs of the person in post as well as satisfying the needs of the LEA.

On the other hand, however, the individually-based career perspective does not exclude the desire for vertical advancement, but nor does it depend upon it. A rewarding career step would be one which provided appropriate levels of 'opportunity' and 'capacity' to fulfil the identification, extension, influence and impact concerns of the teachers. Furthermore, the short-term nature of the job and the fact that its end is not usually the final point in the person's working life means that concerns tend to shift, particularly towards the end of the secondment period. There is a phase of 'taking stock' of what has been learned and how it may be used advantageously in the next post.

Conversations amongst advisory or support teachers who are at different stages in their secondments tend to blur the distinctions between these apparent stages of concern to a greater extent than one might find in a school staffroom. The constant turnover of seconded teachers means that support is required simultaneously for survival needs, for identification, for extension, for evidence of impact and for taking stock of learning. This makes for an intensity of judgments and an acceleration of learning. An additional complexity arises from the fact that the semi-detached teachers are working concurrently in many different school contexts as well as trying to create their own supportive occupational ecology. For this reason the institutional levels of 'capacity' and 'opportunity' are multiple and variable, to the extent that advisory teachers may be striving for survival in their work in one school whilst gaining satisfaction from a sense of impact in another. One major issue which the HMI report on the first year of LEATG scheme (DES, 1989b), failed to mention is that many schools do not, as yet, know how to make best use of support teachers. A recurring theme in the discussions amongst advisory teachers is the way in which they are so often dependent on reluctant teachers and have to work in some school settings which are indifferent or even hostile. This will be addressed in the final chapter on school development. The following ideas, drawing on extracts from evaluation studies, illustrate the kind of concerns being felt by advisory teachers.

The Survival and Identification Concerns of Semi-Detached Teachers

When advisory or support teachers enter a school in a role which has not been clearly defined, it is not surprising that the host and the visiting teachers test each other out as they piece together the clues and signals as to what their work together is going to be about. They are both making sense of a project through the experience of being involved in it. The semi-detached teachers are at the same time striving for some degree of 'competent membership' or identification within the school, and because of this they are easily bruised. In the case of one ESG project, the team of support teachers found it difficult to make personal relationships with the teachers against the background of the 'official' project aims which implied that there was an existing deficit in the schools. It survived by finding ways to be busy without being threatening by:

- Making resources for teachers away from the classroom
- Working with small groups of children either out of the classroom or in a confined corner of the room

- Arranging and helping with visits without any follow-up work
- Covering for teachers so that they may do something else such as visit another school
- Teaching familiar demonstration lessons

Whilst being involved in such fragmented and disconnected, practical activities the team was attempting to build relationships gradually and carefully so that it might eventually begin to influence the teachers' classroom practice and satisfy its own needs to influence and make some impact. The irony was that whilst the support teachers were surviving through being engaged in these safe actvities, they were making themselves vulnerable to criticism from the host teachers:

> [they] take only individual children or small groups out of the classroom . . . . If not teaching they spend time making apparatus — all alone — what bliss, under these conditions we could all make progress and achieve great job satisfaction.

This points to a central tension in the relationship between semi-detached teachers and some of the teachers and school staffs with which they work. The need for identification and 'competent membership' means that the support teachers would like to fit smoothly into the school by being like the host teachers and yet their official position and their exemption from 'normal' school duties and obligations like 'yard duty' suggests that they are different. Furthermore, their very presence implies challenge and change rather than 'settling down' and 'fitting in'. The problem is intensified by the short-term nature of the job. The need for settling-in quietly, conflicts with their feelings of wanting to influence and have some immediate impact on the teachers. The conditions in which this is being attempted, in someone else's school and classroom, make it difficult to keep these needs in a harmonic relationship. The main problem is that these survival strategies of *'being-busy-playing-safe'* may become institutionalized patterns of inter-action which allow host teachers and support teachers to continue to work in a state of truce: in parallel rather than in a learning partnership.

At the same time as they try to fit in to a range of school settings, the support teachers are also attempting to develop an identity as members of the LEA professional service. The difficulty of reconciling the tension between these separate identities was apparent in an ESG project when the team's membership of the steering group and ready access to the LEA adviser and the headteachers led to some unrest amongst some of the host teachers and to some uneasiness on the part of the support teachers themselves. Holly *et al.* (1987) report the reverse problem for the TRIST advisory teachers. As their success in school-based work became evident 'the irony was that the more they became "marginalised . . . boundary figures" within their LEAs. It could be argued that, politically, they were almost "too near to teachers" ' (para. 4.4)

A further problem, which became evident in the whole LEA study, was that the advisers were able to take a longer term view of the task of promoting change. Their timescale might include a succession of advisory teachers 'chipping away' at the obstacles and barriers to change whilst each of the individual support teachers tended to have a greater sense of urgency. The difficulties of achieving a feeling of 'competent membership' within the advisory service were increased during the time when the role of advisory teacher was in the process of being defined in relation to that of a 'full' adviser. This tended to make the distinctions between the posts explicit and to emphasize the 'them and us' differences rather than the similarities. Whilst it was being made clear that the advisory teachers were not 'the Chief Education Officer's representatives' in schools and that their function was narrower than that of the LEA advisers, it was often said that they were able to do the 'real classroom work' which the 'full' advisers would like to do if they were not being diverted to other tasks. Support or advisory teaching was being defined at a time when the main locating job of LEA adviser was itself undergoing change.

It is not surprising then, that the complexity of the semi-detached teacher's occupational identity gives weight to the need for mutual support from colleagues in the same kind of jobs. The TRIST advisory teachers also emphasized the importance of support from external agencies such as higher education institutions. Many evaluators of projects, like myself, have adopted strategies which have involved regular discussions with the support teachers in a way which has helped them to make critical sense of the complexities of their roles.

The Extension Concerns of Semi-Detached Teachers

For mid-career teachers to experience a concern for survival and identification is in itself a form of extension: a learning from reflection on discomfort and challenge. As well as becoming more 'thick-skinned' and developing skills of diplomacy in difficult situations, these experiences, when articulated in the kind of critical discussions referred to above, do have a powerful intensity and immediacy. Semi-detached teachers become astute observers of staffroom and LEA politics. Their collective analysis of their tasks and their problems become sharp and penetrating.

The sense of collegiality of the support teachers became very strong, and reference to teamwork was a recurring theme in all of the data collected. This was what was often said to give them confidence to take risks and to accept that apparent failure was bearable when shared. As one advisory teacher reminded another during a review meeting, the task of approaching teachers was:

— like a game of dares. The four of us sat in our room and said 'Right what are we going to do?' — it was as basic as that, and we'd go through the classrooms and talk about which one we could approach, and we'd say 'She's alright who's going to go?' and I might say, 'I'll go'. I knew that I had the backing of three people and we'd get it all worked out and I'd go. It was a standing joke — I'd be back in five minutes. No good — the most peculiar reasons. Once I was asked, 'Is this interruption really necessary?' I couldn't have done it without the support of the others, it was terrible.

Observation of one large team provided evidence of:

- shared agenda setting;
- collective review of specific problems in the work with a school which, it was thought, affected the whole team; its philosophy, commitments and the robustness of its work;
- reinforcing and nourishing the ideas and principles underlying the work of the group through an attempt to build a conceptual model;
- members reporting on their future plans and inviting others to become involved (in one case, for work with a school which involved several weekend activities);
- a lengthy discussion about the tone of a letter they were writing for schools which revealed a sharp awareness of the delicacy of the relationship between schools and the support service;
- challenging debate about the allocation of tasks, division of labour and recognition which ensues from varied profiles of work.

At the same time, questions were being raised by some advisory teachers about whether a strong team may unwittingly develop an exclusivity through its enhanced 'verbal ability' and confident sense of mission. This was seen as a problem by some who worked as individuals or as weakly allied pairs in the same LEA. Some steps were being taken, at the time of the study, to coordinate the whole service in order to extend the collegiality to all members. What is being suggested, then, is that a period of semi-detachment with the opportunity for collaborative learning with fellow support teachers, offers scope for personal and intellectual extension which may have been unavailable to those who worked in schools with a low 'level of opportunity' (McLaughlin and Yee, 1988) or low 'norms of collegiality and experimentation' (Little, 1982). This will be discussed further in the final chapter, along with an exploration of how the opportunities for coll-aborative learning with teachers in the schools will vary and will depend on the degree to which a 'culture of development' (Holly and Southworth, 1989) already exists.

Impact Concerns of Semi-Detached Teachers

The question of whether or not they are having any impact in influencing the long-term practice of teachers is of major concern to support and advisory teachers. Many become frustrated by the superficiality of some of their work when they sense that it will have little lasting impact. Those participating in the whole LEA study felt that some teachers and schools, and also some of those managing the support service, often underestimated the importance of preparatory groundwork and the subsequent review of classroom work. There were two main facets to the problem of the lack of discussion between the host teachers and the support teachers. Firstly, there was a feeling that this was not seen as 'proper work' and that most of the time spent in a school should be spent in contact with the children in the classrooms. Teaching in classrooms, unlike discussions with teachers, was always seen as a legitimate form of work. It seemed important to be seen to be working hard and not disrupting the normal school arrangements. It felt awkward for an individual advisory teacher to suggest that a teacher would need to be withdrawn for planning and reviewing time. As a consequence, most of the talking was done in snatched time between lessons.

Secondly, there was the issue of how many schools and teachers it was feasible for the support teachers to work with concurrently. In the ESG Primary Science and Technology Project in one LEA there was an attempt to cover all of the schools. This was based on the concepts of justice and fairness, but it tended to reduce the chance of achieving long-term, reflective, learning partnerships with teachers. In this sense, impact was broad but shallow, and other LEA strategies were needed to support the schools which wished to take the development further. Support teachers had to learn 'to drive a fast car'.

One result of being involved in too many concurrent and short-term school contacts and not being able to study long-term progression, was that the support teachers were vulnerable to being over-concerned with immed-iate impact. They became aware of the tendency to favour the dramatic, impressive, set-piece lesson 'which had gone down well before'.

Support teachers seemed to depend on immediate feedback from the classteacher. One significant aspect of this was the enjoyment of a class-teacher's expressed surprise about how well particular children had responded to an activity. This was often said about children with special educational needs whose levels of participation had been greater or better than had been expected. In this way, the support teachers were able to satisfy a need for evidence of classroom impact with specific children even though their knowledge of those children was minimal. They generally put this down to the unwitting way in which they did not communicate negative expectations to the children, as they had no previous knowledge of those children's abilities or attainments.

Discussions between advisory teachers often focused on the question of whether it was more worthwhile to work at some depth in favourable settings or to try to get started where there was perceived inertia or resistance. There was a concern that there was a tendency to 'preach to the converted' or gravitate towards the friendly schools in order to feel that some impact was being made during their period of secondment. Grahame Atkinson takes up this point in Chapter 5 in this volume.

Environmental Factors which Support a Career

McLaughlin and Yee (1988) have listed the characteristics of environments which support a rewarding career as:

> Resource adequate (as opposed to resource deprived)
> Integrated (as opposed to segmented)
> Collegial (as opposed to isolated)
> Problem Solving (as opposed to problem-hiding)
> Investment-centred (as opposed to pay-off focused)

This provides a useful set of criteria against which to consider the extent to which a period of semi-detached and advisory teaching may be a rewarding career phase. It can be argued that most support teachers work in a **resource-adequate** environment. This seems to be especially true of those working on national initiatives such as TVEI and ESG projects. Some dissatisfaction was, however, expressed by some ex-heads of departments from secondary schools who were working on local initiatives and who said that they had less control over ordering than they had in their previous school post. Nevertheless, most of the advisory teachers thought that they had the necessary resources to do their work.

At the time of the study, in one LEA, a truly **integrated environment** had not yet been created in the advisory service, though there were attempts to work toward this and the study itself was evidence of a move towards a unity of purpose, with clear goals and a collective sense of responsibility for the whole service. This raised issues about the degree of uniformity or variation across the different schemes and initiatives. On the one hand, there was the view that support teachers should be closely managed according to an agreed structure with clear parameters, whilst on the other hand, it was suggested that there should be a number of models to suit different purposes and to reflect different values. This represented, to some extent, a tension between the 'control' and 'enabling' aspects, which LEA advisers strive to reconcile in their own work. The former implies hierarchy, standard procedures, routines and uniformity. The latter emphasizes professional autonomy, flexibility and diversity. This tension was most evident, at the time of the study, in the debate about the proportion of time which should be spent in classrooms. It had been suggested that all support teachers should spend 80 per cent of their time in classrooms, but, as mentioned in the first chapter, a survey revealed that the actual time being spent in classrooms varied from 5 per cent to 80 per cent and the ideal time varied between 10 per cent and 80 per cent.

The fact that there was open and extensive discussion about this issue and many others indicates that an attempt was being made to create a **collegial environment**. According to McLaughlin and Yee, this 'enhances the level of opportunity and the level of capacity for teachers, because it serves as a critical source of stimulation and motivation' (p. 34). During the period of the study, the sense of collegiality was increasing rapidly. At first, many of the support teachers had felt isolated and insecure, but a residential conference had provided the first significant move toward the intention of generating professional and social cohesiveness. Apart from this official recognition of its importance, one of the reasons for its rapid development was that it was not assumed that there was a 'correct way' of working. Unlike school staff groups, none of the members had settled down to the comfortable and familiar customs and habits of routine practice. There was no explicit orthodoxy, little dogmatism, and plenty to talk about.

The feeling of all being 'in the same boat' and of all being able to talk about problems without 'losing face' meant that the work environment was **problem-solving** rather than problem-hiding. This encouraged the phenomenon of learning through conversations. The support teachers were becoming more skilful in analysis and reflection rather than competent in set working procedures. Day-to-day problems formed starting points for discussions of fundamental questions about practical ways of promoting and fostering strongly held values about education. At its best it discouraged cautious thinking, it prevented acceptance of superficiality and mediocrity and it led to a tolerance of plurality. One weakness at the time, however, was that the support teachers had not been able to observe each other at work in the schools and classrooms.

The final characteristic cited by McLaughlan and Yee is the **investment-centred** environment. This is contrasted with the 'pay-off' centred environment where getting it right over-and-over again is the most important criterion. The investment-centred environment values growth, risk-taking and change, and it is associated with high levels of opportunity and power. It was evident that the advisory and support teachers valued risk-taking and change, but one of the problems was that they were also aware of inconsistencies in other people's expectations and judgments about their work. They frequently guessed at the implicit criteria by which they were being judged in different schools and in different parts of the LEA. The temptation, in the face of negative feedback or reports of weak practice, is for those managing support teachers to reduce the risk-taking and to introduce routines; to exert greater control through the introduction of rules and restrictions. The challenge for support services in general is to develop enabling forms of evaluation which will increase confidence in terms of building appropriate accountability relationships whilst maintaining the process of learning through reflection and experimentation.

The emphasis which has been placed upon the concept of the individually-based career is not intended to imply that structural change would be unimportant. As is noted in the final chapter it is expected that LEAs will continue to learn more about how to relate advisory teaching to other aspects of their professional services. Furthermore, it is desirable that steps should be taken nationally to facilitate movement between posts in different parts of the education service. This would serve to expand the range of professional learning opportunities for a wider range of teachers.

One of the things which seems to be especially worthwhile about the experience of advisory teaching, however, is that it brings together groups of mid-career teachers who begin to share survival and identification problems through working in new contexts. They find that there are no ready-made routines or orthodoxies, and they tend to support each others' learning by discussing rather than hiding their own concerns. They develop independence in going out alone to work in unfamiliar schools and at the same time they experience the interdependence of being part of their own group.

Personal Accounts

Chapter 4

Working and Learning in Other People's Classrooms

Mike Sullivan

Initial Fears

Secondment for a primary headteacher is a rare occurrence. Mine was not only rare but bordering on the exotic; I was seconded to work as a member of a curriculum support team of eighteen teachers whose base was located on the first floor of my own school. The year was to be spent mainly in schools, supporting initiatives for which the schools had requested help.

The summer months before taking up the secondment were an anxious time. Why had I put my credibility as a teacher and as an organizer to the test? Was it masochism, machoism or sheer madness? Schools that had requested curriculum support were looking for sleeves-rolled-up practical help in implementing ideas in the classroom. How were they going to react to a headteacher who had not had responsibility for a class for the past six years? How was I going to adjust to being one of a new and odd breed of peripatetic support teachers? Schools are well used to having peripatetic teachers that perform a specialist role: the remedial teacher, a musician to take instrumentalists, a member of the language support service to help with E2L work. They flit into schools, perform their designated task and flit out again on a role model sometimes unkindly referred to as 'hit and run'. A headteacher come to develop science, maths, CDT or project work across the curriculum is another matter altogether! What was the role that I was being assigned? What was the role that I wanted to play? What was the role that schools were going to allow me to play? Were my worries just fears of the night or were they substantial? I was soon to find out.

The Experience

One of my earliest attachments was to an infant school. A wary headteacher carefully explained that I would be working under three disadvantages: I was a headteacher, I had never had full-time responsibility for a class of infant children and I was a man! My task, with a colleague from the team, was to support the introduction of a commercial maths scheme. Somehow or other on my first working day I was obliged to take a large middle infant class for PE in the hall. Through an apparently amazing chain of coincidences during the 20 minute lesson, framed in the window of the hall door there appeared in succession the faces of the classteacher, the deputy, the headteacher and the General Inspector of Schools (infant and nursery). We were noisy, we enjoyed ourselves and were puffed out at the end of the lesson. No limbs were broken, there were no tears, no puddles on the floor and no one had run home. It seemed that I had been accredited with some minimum level of competence and from that time on was regarded as safe to be let loose on my own in the school. The first lesson that I had learnt was that establishing credibility as a competent teacher of children was to be an essential and an immediate task in all schools.

Working with headteachers could be a bit tricky. The fact that I was in the school as a support team member and not there with some covert brief was difficult for some to accept. The task was to share ideas and not to act as a mole or supergrass for an inquisitive inspectorate or administration. Indeed, inspectors and administrators were, on the whole, sensitive to the trust and confidentiality of relationships with schools and did not seek 'off the record' impressions.

There was sometimes a mistaken expectation by schools that support team members would play the 'expert' or 'superteach', rubbishing the efforts of the school and producing a wonderful packaged curriculum out of a hat. Even if I had been able to do it I would not have trod that slippery path. The problem of going on an ego trip is the certainty of a trip over the ego. My task was not that of an elixir pedlar but that of supporting the school's efforts with curriculum development, helping with cross-fertilization of ideas, assisting in the identification and provision of adequate resources and last, but not least, to bubble with confident enthusiasm. All attempts at arrogance, bluster, conceit and self-delusion were brutally exposed in the reality of classroom teaching.

Most of my involvements in schools were for one day a week for a term or more and in many cases I shared the assignment with a colleague from the support team. Working in tandem meant that a great deal of flexibility could be built into the system. One team member could be covering a class and the second team member holding discussions with the classteacher. Both the support teachers could cover classes to release a pair of teachers to observe good practice in another school. It was, however, essential that team members serving in tandem in a school had a similar set of beliefs as to what constitutes good practice.

Sharing in detailed curriculum planning with teachers and then having the opportunity to work within classrooms implementing those plans, without the usual disruptions of running a school was marvellous. Establishing relationships within staff rooms was fairly easy; contributing to, but not dominating curriculum meetings, needed commonsense and a modicum of tact. Working in classrooms was a different and rather harder proposition. Who was in charge of the classroom, the classteacher or the floating head? Who was to take the lead in teaching? Who would carry tales back to the head's office?

There was frequently a sense of unease by the classteachers as to why they had been singled out for 'support'. Was it because their teaching was regarded as inadequate, or because they were the 'soft target' on the staff? If the 'support' was to help with the introduction of a new scheme or a new curriculum area, then the unease was less than in the development of an established area such as project work. The first reaction of many classteachers was to offer a group that I could work with outside; another classroom, the hall, the corridor, the moon, in fact anywhere where I could not overlook the classroom teacher at work with children. It took a great deal of trust and acceptance from teachers to get in alongside them in the classroom. Often the work was hardly developed further than parallel teaching which was useful in that the classteacher and I could keep an eye on what each other was doing and feed off each other's skills. Debriefing and planning sessions were essential so that we could evaluate the success or otherwise of the teaching strategies that we were employing. I was very conscious of the relentless, conflicting pressures and demands on teachers' attention and time. Discussion seemed invariably to focus on practical problems and short-term objectives rather than exploring long-term goals and the theory underlying the work.

There were occasions when everything was just right. Confidence and professional compatibility were such that the exchange of ideas and the development of appropriate teaching and learning strategies took off, leading to a string of new perceptions and the acquisition of new skills. It was definitely a two-way process. Work on science with gifted infant teachers certainly caused me to lift my expectations of children's performance and understanding.

There were a small minority of schools where relationships between staff members were strained and in some cases openly hostile. In such circumstances there was always the danger of being sucked into the whirlpool of internal school politics and feuding. This was a particular hazard where headteachers had allowed themselves to become isolated from their staffs. The 'what do you think?' and 'what would you do?' type of questions on general management issues could be particularly barbed and needed sensitive handling.

One interesting activity in staff rooms was to identify the opinion makers. There were usually one or two people on each staff that exerted a strong influence on the ethos and working practices of the school. The natural leaders were not always those that held the highest positions in the management structure of the school and could include the school secretary and ancillary assistants. The natural leaders were the keys to making an involvement a success or reducing it to a dismal failure.

Clearly my task was to help bring about change. This presented challenges to established systems of teaching, organization and management. Individual power bases of expertise, knowledge and skills were sometimes threatened, as were status and personal control of resources. Unless one was quick to recognize the stake that individuals had in a system so that allowances, trade-offs and status protection could be at least considered, and if possible negotiated, then obstructive tactics and sheer bloody-mindedness could be encountered. My role was not only to help schools bring about change, but to do this in a way that was as painless and as productive as possible. This could only be brought about by working through others; winning friends and influencing people was a prime activity.

Making Effective Use of Support Teachers

Classroom-based support is an expensive and limited luxury that can easily be squandered unless great care is taken in the way that the support is planned, executed and monitored. The whole business of negotiating support, the wheeling and dealing, is a tricky activity. Exploring people's perceptions of what can be provided, what will be provided, what is realistic and what is idealistic takes time and effort but if the match isn't right from the beginning then disappointments and misunderstandings will inevitably follow.

Discovering the source of requests for support is one of the first tasks to be undertaken. Is it just the headteacher looking for some strong arm characters to put members of staff into line or to carry out initiatives that he or she should be able to do on their own? Is it perceived as an opportunity for the headteacher to make his or her name as someone at the forefront of developments? Is it a gimmick, a bee in the bonnet or is it a genuine perceived need shared by the staff, something they really want to do? It is on these issues that the willingness of staff to be involved will depend.

The requests for help were sometimes vague, causing wonder about the amount of preliminary consultation and discussion that had taken place. When the intentions of the school were not clear then opportunity cost had not been taken into consideration. Project and topic work, for example, were prime areas where help was requested by schools without enough time given to initial preparation. Alongside ambitious schemes for topic and project work, history, geography and science were often still timetabled with the result that the curriculum would be fragmented and overcrowded.

Curriculum change is not only about taking on new areas but also giving up others. One of the difficult aspects about choosing between alternatives is that there is always opportunity cost, to attempt to stuff even more into the curriculum means that the quality of experience suffers. It seems to me that the most effective involvements were where staff were committed and enthusiastic to bring about change, where the headteacher was fully involved and not just giving benevolent encouragement and where there was some idea of time scale. There had been a review carried out by the staff of a curriculum area and as a consequence of the review the majority of staff shared a belief that change was necessary. Consultation had taken place with the Pastoral Inspector. Options had been generated and consequences considered. Long- and short-term plans had been sketched out including speculative 'if — then' options about the use of support team members. The support team leader had negotiated with the headteacher the general details of time input and checked the feasibility of plans. Detailed preliminary discussions between headteacher, individual teachers and team members would follow. Often classteachers would regard these 'lead in' discussions as a waste of time! It was when these preliminaries were skimped and the level of preparation was low that the real waste of time took place.

In these successful involvements there were also carefully negotiated written contracts clearly giving everyone an idea of the roles that they were to play. It was a game of consequences which had a ripple effect touching all members of the school even when the work of team members was restricted just to two or three classrooms.

Who should have the responsibility of monitoring curriculum development and the ways in which support is used? There is always a risk of failure or misuse of support teacher time. It can be a temptation for a hard pressed headteacher to attempt to use support teachers as supply cover when the going gets tough! The team leader has a crucial role to play in resolving both major and minor problems of this sort. A team leader needs to have the authority and the power to pull team members out of a school when things aren't going well. To say that it's not working, this isn't right, let's postpone it, let's come back later when things are clearer, when people have had chance to think things through. Muddling through just wouldn't do. Good communication is vital, not only between team members and the members of staff with which they are working but also with all members of staff within the school, the Pastoral Inspector, the team leader and with other interested bodies. Some headteachers took the opportunity to invite support team members to speak at governors' meetings about the work that they had undertaken.

One of the preoccupations of any involvement is about the continuation of initiatives after the support teachers are withdrawn. If the initiative is not robust enough to be self-sustaining or the project has been organized so that it can only flourish with the extra staffing and expertise provided through team members then obviously planning and the execution of the involvement has failed. There is always risk of failure in an involvement and without careful monitoring the risk is compounded.

Lessons Learned

The secondment was in many ways like a very long teaching practice. There was always critical professional interest in what one was doing and saying, both in and outside the classroom. The activities that were assigned to the children, the workcards and worksheets had to be well matched and well presented. Impromptu entertainments and time fillers just would not do.

One of the things that needed to be learnt very quickly was accurate and comprehensive note-taking. It was too easy for me to become confused over long-term goals and short-term objectives particularly when providing support in the same curriculum area in two different schools. Without an adequate system of note-taking and referral, promises made to provide materials or to gather information from specialist sources would be unkept.

I enjoyed working in other people's schools; there was a cross-fertilization of ideas, I developed new enthusiasms and knowledge. The achievements and problems of my own school were seen in a wider perspective. Moreover, I think the staff of my own school had changed in my absence; relationships are now different, for we had to live for 12 months without depending on each other and have grown stronger and refreshed for the experience. Each member of the staff undertook extra and different responsibilities gaining new insights into the organization of the curriculum and management of the school. There is a reaffirmation that our march onward is no forced march to the beat of a single drum.

The curriculum support team was physically located in part of my own school so that I remained attached to it; there was always a sense of belonging and the sense that I would be returning. There is a sense of continuity and security that many ESG (Education Support Grant) funded advisory teachers, and teachers in detached services don't enjoy. I'm not quite sure who gained most from the secondment, the schools that I was supposed to be assisting, my own school or whether in fact I scooped the pool.

Chapter 5

Cosy or Critical Classroom Support?
'Having you there to share in the problems I was facing.'

Graham Atkinson

> . . . It certainly gave me more confidence having you there to share
> in the problems I was facing. Because I think, very often, if you're
> in the classroom and you're trying something new, even if you go
> afterwards and talk to somebody about what's happened, it's not
> always the same as having somebody in the classroom who is
> sharing the same things as they are happening.

The aim of this chapter is to reflect upon my own practice as a support
teacher for Integrated Humanities; identifying, where able, contradictions
and issues which might enable me to modify aspects of my working. I will
investigate the relationships between myself, as a support teacher, and a
classteacher, with whom I was working in a team teaching situation, since
such relationships are fundamental to the quality of my work. I shall make
particular reference to the principle of student-centred learning (Brandes
and Ginnis, 1986). Student-centred learning (SCL) has a number of guiding
principles, which I will identify, that might transpose from one learning
context to another, and in this case I would like to establish to what degree
those principles were present in my own practice, and what issues this raises.
In this instance, the participants have clearly separate roles and
responsibilities, and I should like to consider certain issues pertaining to my
role, as a support teacher, that emerge from this. I shall consider the role of a
support teacher as that of a 'teacher leader' (Lieberman, 1988), and seek to
clarify what implication this might have for the development of my role and
the context within which I function.

Establishing Working Arrangements

I began working directly with this particular teacher in September of 1988. I first met her on the day of her appointment to her present school, over a term previously, when I offered support, should it be wanted. (I am not sure what her perception of 'support' was at that time.) A number of meetings allowed us to become better acquainted, though there was no request for support. Toward the end of her first term at her new school the teacher was to attend a course on SCL. I was able to lend her some appropriate literature and said I would be interested to hear her views following the course. Subsequently, having suggested the possibility of classroom support, should she be considering any experimental work with SCL, we agreed to work together in her classroom. Our aim was to attempt to work in a *more explicitly* student-centred way than the teacher had previously felt able to do, and to allow both the teacher and myself to continue to develop together as teachers and deepen our understanding of the practice of SCL. The subject area in which we were to work was Integrated Humanities.

I have come to recognize the need to negotiate expectations and procedures as a fundamental to classroom-based support. Thus, prior to beginning work in the classrom, the teacher and I discussed at length what we intended to do and how we might approach it. In this case there was a complication with the addition of another group to the original group of students. This was a group of students with special educational needs which had previously been segregated. A decision had been taken, at departmental level, which meant that they would join our group whilst working on the first unit of their humanities course. This, in effect, meant that they joined our group for the first term's work. More significantly, this group was accompanied by the special educational needs (SEN) teacher who normally had independent responsibility for them. This teacher had no specific knowledge of SCL, though she expressed an interest and a willingness to participate. Initially, since I was felt to have greater experience in the practice of SCL, it was decided that I might lead the first sessions both as a means of introducing myself to the whole group and of introducing the idea of working in a different way to the students. I was concerned not to present a demonstration lesson, and responsibility for subsequent lessons was to be either shared or taken in turn. The additions to the original group of students and the addition of a colleague who had not been 'in' from the outset were to raise some issues which had to be addressed.

I worked with the group for two sessions each week. This meant that I was present during all of their humanities lessons and was regarded as one of the teachers, though still a visitor. The pattern of working followed a previously agreed structure in which the host teacher took responsibility for the content to be presented, the process being discussed at meetings before each lesson. The teacher and I would then review the week's sessions and consider the coming week's work. The SEN teacher was invited to all meetings but was often not present. (I will discuss implications of this in a later section.)

Early sessions focused upon turning what were two separate groups into one group:

Classteacher: I think that we needed those first four weeks . . . the pupils sort of accepted each other.

Classteacher: About half way through the term I felt I wished I hadn't spent as long on the getting to know each other . . . but I think, looking back, I'm very glad we did spend the time doing that.

Time was spent on exercises to establish ground rules and to get to know one another. The term was interrupted by a TVEI week, with three days residential and two days experience-based learning in school. All but a few of the students went to stay at a YMCA hostel and take part in outdoor activities and visits related to their humanities course. Following this, work was directed towards the assignments which were required for the GCSE. By end of term, the Christmas events in school and the completion of the assignments brought the formalized working to an end.

Following such an involvement with a colleague it has been my practice to meet and reflect upon the work, hoping to draw out major points relating to our learning, and considering the future. In this instance, since I was looking to record evidence of my own work for use in this enquiry, I asked the teacher if I might formalize the review and tape record our discussions for this purpose. The teacher has been given a copy of the transcript and we have discussed various drafts of this chapter.

Student-Centred Learning and Teacher Leadership

I would now like to clarify the principles of SCL, as I understand them, and also the idea of teacher leadership, before bringing them to bear upon this discussion of my role.

The term 'student-centred learning' was introduced by Carl Rogers (Rogers, 1983). My understanding and my own practice in SCL have mainly been developed in my own classroom as a consequence of reading *A Guide to Student-Centred Learning* (Brandes and Ginnis, 1986), and having worked with Donna Brandes on several occasions through her involvement with the TVEI project.

The main principle of SCL, as identified by Brandes and Ginnis, is that:

The learner has full responsibility for her own learning.

This is about, what is currently often termed, the ownership of learning. It addresses the issue of who controls the learning. It is one principle which I believe to be of great importance in establishing the other principles, which are stated as follows:

The subject matter has relevance and meaning.
The involvement and participation are necessary for learning.
The relationship between learners is significant.
The teacher becomes a facilitator and resource person.
The learner sees himself or herself differently as a result of the learning experience.
The learner experiences confluence in his or her education.

Perhaps two areas which require clarification are those which refer to 'the relationship between learners' and to 'confluence'.

In the relationshp between the learners, emphasis is placed upon the quality of the interaction, not accepting that dialogue and/or interaction are enough in themselves, but also seeking to develop trust and empathy. Specifically, Brandes and Ginnis talk of the 'helping relationship' and they identify a goal for SCL as enabling people to make their own choices. In raising the idea of 'confluence' they suggest that the present emphasis upon the cognitive domain, and the tendency to neglect the effective domain, should be modified. Thinking and feeling should 'flow together' in the learning process. Questions then arise concerning the relative values placed upon them and whether they can be attended to separately. Is there a need for greater disclosure of feelings in working relationships? The implications of this in the professional relationships between teaching colleagues could also be significant, considering the present isolationist culture of teaching, and the sensitivities relating to autonomy (Hargreaves, 1982), where open and/or honest expressions of feelings are not readily made.

I encountered the ideas of *teacher leadership* in my readings when looking at my role as a support teacher. It is a concept which appears to shift the emphasis, from meeting institutional, parental and student needs, to meeting the needs of teacher colleagues, supporting them in their efforts to meet the professional demands made upon them. I interpret this to mean a teacher whose first concern is to care about other teachers and their teaching. In their chapter on the ideology and practice of teacher leadership,

Lieberman *et al.* (1988) discuss the skills which teacher leaders bring to the role and, also, the necessary on-the-job learning which allows them to cope with their new positions. The need to be an experienced *learner*, along with possessing experience and expertise as a teacher, seems to be paramount in coming to terms with such roles.

> It is important to note that although these people were very experienced, they learned from both their new role and the context of their particular program.

Later in the chapter, they highlight a number of characteristic themes relating to the structure of schools and ways of working with colleagues:

> Placing a non-judgmental value on providing assistance.
> Modelling collegiality as a mode of work.
> Enhancing teachers' self-esteem.
> Using different approaches to assistance.
> Building networks of human and material resources for the school community.
> Creating support groups for school members.
> Making provisions for continuous learning and support for teachers at the school site.
> Encouraging others to take leadership roles with their peers.

It is not my intention in this chapter to explore in detail the implications of the above, but I see links between the principles of SCL and these reorganized characteristics of teacher leadership, especially as they have influenced my practice as a support teacher.

Whose Learning Agenda?

The data I am using is an entire transcript of a conversation with the teacher with whom I had established the team-teaching. We were in fact a team of three, and a clear omission from this review is the SEN teacher, with whom we both worked. This highlights the need to consciously induct colleagues into new situations. This was attempted but, perhaps, only in a token way and insufficient time and care was taken to allow the re-negotiation of aims and, thus, a sense of joint control. The consequence of this was that, although working alongside us in the classroom, the SEN teacher did not take part in the review process.

To collect data, I chose to use interview as conversations were already a regular part of our working relationship. The difference on this occasion was

that the process became formalized, in that I structured my questioning
beforehand. In consultation with another support teacher, I developed a
number of lines of questioning. The aim was to offer the teacher an
opportunity to reflect upon her recent practice, within a structure, with the
intention of making explicit what progress she felt she had made. It was not
for the purpose of generating issues or challenging perceptions, but to
reinforce the aspects of development which were valued by the teacher. I did
not set out to evaluate the support role though this was a part of the work
under review. Before considering the data from the interview, I should like
to consider some of the issues raised when examining the context of the
interview.

Support work is not just about helping, which may infer a deficiency on
the part of a colleague. It ought to imply mutuality. This echoes the
principle of 'modelling collegiality' through 'support teaching'. These ideas
and interpretations of my role have developed through my work. Some
colleagues, sharing a similar position, have developed different
understandings of 'support'. To some degree, there is evidence in the
interview, principally through the tenor of it, to suggest that the teacher and
I shared a perception of 'support', through working on the project. I have no
record, however, of what perception of 'support' might have prevailed
before it became defined in practice. This point will be developed later when
I consider what the implications of my role are in terms of my relationship
with teacher colleagues. What are the factors which determine where and
with whom I am to work? Do these factors pose questions relating to my
assumptions about my working? Given that I was free to decide where I
worked and that there were adequate alternative activities available, why did
I choose this project? By choosing to work with one colleague, do I deny
opportunities to another with greater need? What is the process of the
selection of working partnerships?

The first part of the interview sought to 're-establish the purpose of
support'. The project had started as a consequence of a number of meetings
where common interests were identified:

> *Support teacher*: I was looking for some way of bringing in a more
> students-centred approach, and it just happened that
> the conversation I had with you, talking about what
> you did with [name of school] . . . fitted in with the
> ideas I was having for the humanities . . .

It seemed, on reflection, that I may have been seeking to continue my own
development prior to my return to classroom teaching by experimenting
with student-centred principles. What I did was to find a colleague who was

prepared to share her classroom with me, for this purpose. Was I trying to minimize risk in what is a risk-taking job, by selecting colleagues with whom 'success' is more likely?

The above issues about the 'selection procedure' for support, leads me to discuss the principle of ownership, and thus control of the learning. If my own learning-needs implicitly shaped the selection of the project, did they also usurp the project itself? In considering this, I returned to discuss the development of the relationship between myself and the classteacher. Each meeting, prior to the project, was *potentially* for negotiation of the terms of the project. This is because, in my role, I am presently considering the possibility that each relationship with a colleague (in my case within the humanities) is, or ought to be, essentially supportive. Thus the importance of a negotiated definition of 'support'. By the time that 'support' has achieved the stage of a collaborative activity, and if the negotiation/relationship has been successful, then there should be a shared understanding. This would mean that the ownership of the work can be genuinely shared by the participants.

In the interview, the teacher refers to the fact that she was looking for some way of introducing SCL and she had heard of a previous project of mine, which 'fitted in with my new types of ideas'. Later in the interview she says how having been 'reasonably convinced', following a course, 'I was given the opportunity by the fact that you were able to come and work with me'. Throughout, the use of 'I' and 'we' reassures me that the ownership of our learning was being, to some extent, shared. The main issue being that the SEN teacher was probably excluded, perhaps inevitably, since she had not been part of the 'negotiated definition of support'.

This last point takes me to the principle of 'the relationship between teachers as learners'. The SEN teacher had not had the opportunity to 'own' the project. She was not mentioned during the interview until the very end where she is acknowledged for her expertise. I do not believe it is intended to be dismissive, but, clearly her presence was not identifiable in the review of the project. The relationship between myself and the classteacher had become supportive. For instance, when I raised a matter about my classroom credibility, following an incident with some students in her group, she took pains to reassure me. Similarly, there is evidence that the teacher did experience a genuine feeling of support in the classroom:

Classteacher: I don't know if you realize, but it gave me a lot of confidence just to have you there, knowing that there was somebody else to turn to . . . if it all turned into a riot and disaster, or something like that . . . I'd blame you! (laughs)

The humour, in context, hints at the genuineness and indicates the trust which exists between us, and equally it also conveys a way in which a support teacher can help colleagues to take risks.

In structuring the review, the idea of sustaining, even promoting self-esteem, in line with the principles of student-centred learning and 'teacher leadership', was a specific focus, and thus, the development of appropriate lines of questioning was important. The interview was semi-structured in the sense that I decided that I would try to confine questioning, once a topic was initiated, to reflecting back comments and to seeking clarification. The aim of this was to allow the teacher to determine the agenda, but within a number of specific areas which were made clear from the beginning. The fact that the review process was determined and regulated by myself raises questions about the control, ownership and purpose of the review. Some questions were more successful than others in developing a particular line of . discussion. For example, when I sought to summarize a comment it seemed to invite agreement rather than develop a line of thought, as when I suggested 'planning in the planning' in response to the teacher returning to this particular concern:

> (I had just initiated a new topic. The cassette had come to end and, having turned it over, I reminded the teacher of the topic, which was about one of the students we worked with.)
>
> *Support teacher*: John Smith? Right.
>
> *Classteacher*:   I was just going to say about the planning. It was alright me saying that I would have felt happier if we had planned in advance, but it was all so new, I don't know if it would have been possible to plan in advance.
>
> *ST*:   So it is almost a case of saying you plan in the planning!
>
> *CT*:   Yes.
>
> *ST*:   Does that make sense?
>
> *CT*:   Yes. Yes.
>
> *ST*:   I'm interested in John because . . .
>
> (Clearly, I got my way.)

Although the teacher had brought discussion back to this point, the summary seems to end that line of thought without opportunity for further exploration of the concern. Consequently, I think that, in an interview of this nature, asking a further question, rather than summarizing, may be a better policy.

The above point, about whether it would have been possible to plan in advance, contradicts an earlier statement regarding the planning of the project, where the idea that everything should have been done in advance was proposed.

> I felt that if instead of having planning meetings...every Monday, I think I would have preferred to have done it beforehand. I think that would have got a lot of my anxieties away...

This underlines the tension between the planning, serving to confine the learning experience by not leaving sufficient flexibility to respond to the unexpected, and the need to plan for personal security and to direct and control the quality of the learning.

A question which later concerned me was when I had asked, '...did you consider student relationships previously in your teaching?' The answer is initially 'Yes, I did.' The teacher then responded by illustrating this point, listing various informal activities undertaken with students. Such a question infers that the teacher may not have considered student relationships previously and it seems to prompt a defensive response. In the main, I controlled the agenda by selecting the topics which I wished to develop or on occasion, as in the earlier example on planning, directing the conversation towards areas which interested me. I thought I was helping the teacher to focus upon particular aspects of her learning, and until I had analyzed the transcript a number of times, I remained under the impression that the teacher was in control. This again emphasizes the problematic nature of 'ownership'.

One purpose of the support role is to help classroom teachers to take risks which challenge prevailing orthodoxies:

> *Classteacher*: I was quite frightened that as soon as I went over to student-centred learning...it was as if I was going from one end to the other...I think the big thing I had was the talking in class. And now I can't think how I could have had so many silent classes, and have thought that that was a good thing.

When introducing this chapter, I pointed out that I believed that in respect to control the teacher and I had separate roles and responsibilities. Also in introducing the concept of 'teacher leadership' I stated that leadership roles required a shift of emphasis: to focus specifically upon the needs of teacher colleagues. During our project, the teacher was, as usual, concerned with issues of control,

> . . . that's only just come to me now. That discipline and control was such a big thing in my life . . .

and assessment,

> I was still worried how I was going to assess these discussions that we were having. How was I going to assess their simulation work . . . very much it wasn't as individual, it was a group.

My responsibility was to support the teacher through these uncertainties, and to help sustain our focus upon the classroom processes, their implementation and review. I endeavoured to make my principal concern the classteacher, and so assist her to focus upon the aims of our project despite the significant and important distractions which occurred. Stenhouse (1975), when discussing the process model of curriculum, states that:

> The conditions of teaching at present too often make survival a more urgent concern than scholarship. And more research and development is needed to forge teaching procedures which embody survival techniques compatible with the personal and intellectual development of both pupils and teachers.

Support teaching, where colleagues have equally important but different responsibilities, may offer scope for such classroom research and development.

Support Teaching and Action Research

I would now like to come to the relationship between this project, my work and action research, whilst attempting to identify key methodological issues which arose during this enquiry into my practice.

The nature of my role, the process of review undertaken and the form of enquiry suggest what Carr and Kemmis (1986) define as the 'practical' action research approach, in as much as it is the educational perspectives of the teachers 'that provide the reference point for inquiries' and that it 'seeks to change practice by feeding practical wisdom'. My own role, in this case, might be interpreted as that of 'the teacher as researcher' (Stenhouse, 1975); not in my own classroom, though broadly within classroom practice. I realize I have become one step removed from Stenhouse's original idea of cooperative research by teachers using full-time researchers in support, but the focus upon the teaching, the added advantage of time within which to reflect and the access which a support teacher can have to research facilities means the role may be a route to establish effective links between full-time researchers and the classroom.

Although the transcript of the interview and this chapter have been given to the teacher with whom I was working, my patterns of working and the length of my contract mean that I have been unable to participate further, in any formal sense. The collaboration has ended, though the dialogue has continued. This leads to a conclusion that there would be advantages in basing 'support' teachers within a school. This would offer the opportunity for continuity. On the basis of previous work, new activity could be negotiated; hopefully, deepening the enquiry and focusing on issues identified in the earlier work. This might generate the potential to move further along the action-research continuum towards a 'critical' approach, because as a school staff becomes collectively more experienced in researching its own practices, it is more likely to engage in dialogue, not only within itself, but also with external partners. Carr and Kemmis (1986) state:

> The aim of critical action-research, therefore, is to establish self critical communities in which teachers can reflect on the way in which their own ideas and beliefs may operate to maintain non-educational forms of practice . . .

The function of the recorded data was to provide a source of ideas for subsequent conversation about the issues which emerged from the enquiry, from both of our points of view. Future research of this nature might benefit from accompanying field notes, and possibly a diary. Asking others with appropriate experience, preferably a 'critical community', to consider the transcript of the interview, once it was anonymous, would also have raised issues unseen by myself and the classteacher.

What Were the Implications of this Enquiry for My Practice?

In some ways the enquiry reinforced previous learning. For example, the need to negotiate ground rules when working with colleagues. It prompts me to further investigate the support role, the idea of the separation of responsibilities and the concept of 'teacher leadership' as a means of fostering teacher development. Access to development opportunity, for myself, is now an issue in my work. I am now asking to what degree support for teachers should be conditional.

Currently, there is plenty to be done with those colleagues with whom I can more easily agree a programme of work, without seeking out colleagues who are resistant to change. The prerequisite, for my involvement with a colleague, is that I am **invited**, by that colleague, to work in his or her classroom. There needs to be a culture within schools which makes use of support (Lieberman *et al.*, 1988), but can the creation of 'safe' environments help to create critical communities? Giroux (1981) makes this point very clearly when discussing what he terms strategy-based radicalism:

> Under such circumstances, 'personal warmth, trust and community' become solipsistic categories that deny the intersubjective realms of morality and history. Self indulgence becomes synonymous with liberation, and the privatized morality of the classroom becomes an effective antidote for the moral complexities and political problems that characterize the society at large. In brief, the systematic, boring socialization of the classroom gives way to a 'radical' socialization, warmth and personal autonomy — may appear more palatable, but, in the final analysis may be no less 'oppressive'.

I have quoted this at length because it is a position to which I am sympathetic, and is indicative of the concerns I have relating to my own practice as a support teacher. Is my way of supporting both students and teacher colleagues, only the offering of a palliative and does it obstruct the development of genuinely critical approaches? Is it cosy or is it critical?

Learning Together in the Classroom

Chapter 6

Collaborative Action Research: Working Together Towards Professional Development

---

Bridget Somekh

Introduction: From My Own Experience

As a beginning teacher I often felt alone. In reality, I was continuously with students between the ages of 11 and 18, trying to respond to a stream of questions and requests, talking almost all the time . . . but I felt isolated. I also had a strong sense that my personality was under attack. In the classroom and around the corridors and playgrounds I found myself required to adopt behaviour patterns which went against my image of the kind of person I wanted to be. Every evening and at the weekends I faced a large amount of marking and preparation, some of which I tried to squeeze into school hours by sitting by myself in the quiet area of the staffroom. I felt I never quite fitted the social scene, although I grasped at any opportunity to attend meetings and engage in discussion about my work. Gradually I became aware of inexplicable currents of antagonism which I put down to my own ineptitude in dealing with colleagues. In fact, I was working in a stressed environment. Everyone expended untold care on the students because it was a school with a strongly articulated child-centred philosophy — but we didn't care in the same way for each other. We thought we didn't have time.

This experience will have a ring of truth for most teachers. It has been well documented by Nias (1985, pp. 3–25) who writes of the 'individual [teacher's] continuing concern . . . for the preservation of his/her self image'; and Rogers (1983, p. 9) who quotes an outstanding teacher, Mike, who is leaving teaching because:

> The school is adopting policies I can't live with . . . and besides, the other members of the teaching staff don't really like what I am doing.

I didn't realize it at the time but my experience represents one aspect of the

Figure 6.1 Action research as a series of cycles (*reprinted from Elliott, 1983, p.3*)

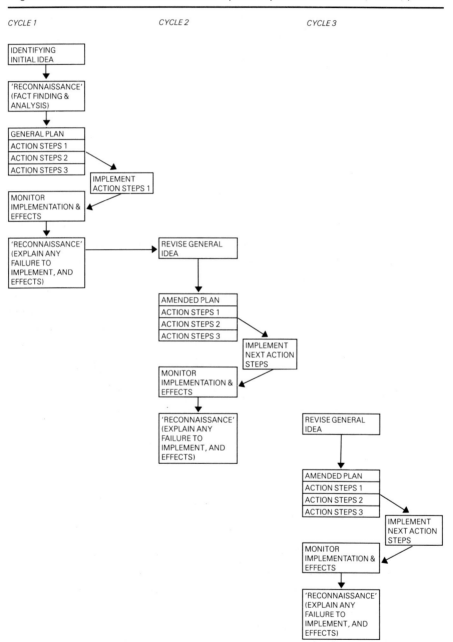

social reality of teaching, although there are obviously variations to the pattern in different schools. Isolation is probably the single most important factor which inhibits the professional development of teachers.

This book takes as its theme the need to break down isolation. It is about teachers building support and working together. The particular purpose of this chapter is to describe a method of collaboration, action research, which focuses on the professional development of the teachers concerned.

Action Research: Practitioner Research Geared to Action

Action Research is distinguished from other educational research by two factors: (i) it is carried out by teachers themselves rather than being research carried out *on* teachers by outsiders; and (ii) its results are fed back directly into the classroom so that immediate action can be taken if the teacher/researcher feels it is appropriate. It is, therefore, eminently practical rather than theoretical; and it deals with the specific circumstances of *this* classroom here and now rather than any hypothetical average classroom. Elliott (1983, p. 3), building on the work of Lewin as developed by Kemmis (1989), presents action research as a series of cycles involving fact finding and analysis, action steps and evaluation, as set out in the diagram presented as Figure 6.1.
He stresses the dynamic and flexible quality of action research:

> The general idea should be allowed to shift.

> 'Reconnaissance' should involve analysis as well as fact finding, and should constantly recur in the spiral of activities, rather than occur only at the beginning.

> 'Implementation' of an action-step is not always easy, and one should not proceed to evaluate the effects of an action until one has monitored the extent to which it has been implemented.

There have been several important research projects in Britain involving teachers in action research, notably the Ford Teaching Project,[1] the Teacher Pupil Interaction and the Quality of Learning Project,[2] and the Teaching, Handling Information and Learning Project.[3] Currently, Pupil Autonomy in Learning with Microcomputers,[4] involves teachers in thirty schools in Cambridgeshire, Essex and Norfolk. A considerable amount of action research has also been carried out by teachers studying for Advanced

Diplomas and Higher Degrees. Other studies have been carried out by teachers working either alone or in small groups, supported by organizations such as the Classroom Action Research Network[5] or by higher education institutions.

Action research is important because it enables teachers to participate directly in curriculum research and development. Defining the central problem of curriculum study as 'the gap between our ideas and aspirations and our attempts to operationalize them', Stenhouse (1975, p. 3) writes:

> The gap can be closed only by adopting a research and development approach to one's own teaching, whether alone or in a group of co-operating teachers.

Thus, if we agree with Stenhouse, the curriculum received by children is wholly dependent on the teachers who deliver it; and involving teachers in action research is one of the most effective ways of closing the gap between aspiration and practice and ensuring that real curriculum development takes place. The corollary of this is that action research enables the professional development of teachers by allowing them to control their own learning and match it exactly to their own needs. Within action research, curriculum development, teacher professional development and research are combined in a single process.

Action research is essentially a collaborative process and therefore of particular interest in combating the professional isolation of teachers. Although the researcher *is* the practitioner, it has been found that an outsider can be crucially important as an assistant, or **facilitator**, to the research process. At its simplest level this is because there is a problem in being a participant observer in social interaction if your role in the interaction is a central one. Most of the famous participant observation studies (see, for example, Whyte's, 1955, pp. 299–307, study of Cornerville) have allowed the researcher to cast herself/himself in the role of a naive member of the group, able to spend a considerabale part of the time collecting information. Teachers only have the luxury of adopting that role in special circumstances. An outsider/facilitator can assist as an observer or interviewer, contribute a fresh, impartial view and talk through analysis of the issues. Although not the researcher, the facilitator can become heavily involved in the research process. Working in partnership the teacher and outsider/facilitator can regulate the exact nature of each's involvement in the research. This relationship is often described as that of a teacher/researcher and **critical friend**.

Barriers to Building Support / Advisory Relationships

Perhaps one could distinguish between support teachers and advisory teachers by saying that the former are primarily there to supplement the teaching given to the students, while the latter are primarily there to support the professional development of the teacher. In either case, the establishment of a supportive working relationship with the teacher is crucially important. Some further analysis of the reasons for teacher isolation may help to indicate possible barriers to establishing this relationship.

I was very much struck by my former colleague, Colleen McLaughlin's, description of teaching as 'the most publicly performed private act'. For me it is the key to why, as a beginning teacher, I felt my personality was under attack. Schools are not free institutions. They begin and end with roll calls as a check that the students have fulfilled their legal obligation to attend. As Stenhouse (1975, p. 167) points out, schools and some armed forces are alike in asking professionals to work with unwilling conscripts. This is presumably the root of some of the rules laid down by schools: some are to ensure that anti-social behaviour does not take place (no chewing gum, no running in the corridor), and others are to provide demonstrable evidence that authority is fully accepted (no unusual cuts or colours of hair, no wearing of coats in lessons). In David Lodge's novel, *Ginger You're Barmy* (1962, p. 87), the protagonist withdraws his application to become an officer and says in explanation:

> I suppose it's my education. I've been encouraged to question everything, to form an independent judgement. In the Army one has to accept orders without questioning them. I feel that if I were to hope to become an officer I would have to give up too many principles.

Teachers are unable to withdraw unless they leave the profession. By default they have to accept the officer's role as leader and controller of both the willing and the unwilling. They choose between becoming fierce disciplinarians or becoming skilled performers who can hold their audience's attention willingly. They become skilled at negotiating with the students, adapting their behaviour to get the most positive response demanded by the majority. Chameleon-like, they adopt slightly different behaviour patterns with different class groups. At the same time teachers work in institutions which specialize in testing, grading and assessing performance. It is a small step from expecting a lot of their pupils to expecting a lot of themselves. Furthermore, teaching is a highly skilled and complex activity which can never be wholly successful (if you define success in terms of achieving what you set out to achieve) because students are individuals and bring to the learning process their own biases and interests. In the final analysis, teachers are limited to communicating through language which can only ever approximate to what they mean and is open to quite different interpretations by each listener: to hope to communicate effectively with thirty people at once is a tall order, even supposing you have captured their full attention! The classroom, therefore, is an intensely intimate environment in which teachers are conscious of performing unnaturally, and in which they continually compromise their ideals and suffer the stress of a sense of partial failure. It follows that they are very unwilling to perform in front of other adults, including colleagues whose own teaching they may assume to be unproblematic.

The move towards appointing a substantial number of support and advisory teachers is built on the premise that breaking down the isolation of the classroom is extremely helpful in the professional development of teachers. However, what seems at first the relatively unproblematic step of placing in-service and curriculum support in the classroom in the form of another teacher, actually threatens teachers' professional confidence . . . and this needs to be addressed if the support strategy is to be effective.

Shaking the Kaleidoscope: A New View of Teacher Professionalism

The isolation of many teachers is, therefore, largely due to the concept of what it is to be a teacher. It has been nurtured by the expectations of students who expect the teacher to be an authority in terms of both control and knowledge; and by teacher trainers who observe lessons on teaching practice and write critiques of performance; and even by colleagues who bolster their own confidence by making tacit comparisons . . . so that there is an unhealthy gleam of interest when problems are confided. Another view is possible with a shake of the kaleidoscope.

Donald Schon (1983) develops an alternative view of what it means to be a professional. By observing the practice of a designer, a psychiatrist, a lawyer and others, he effectively challenges the notion of the professional as someone with specialist knowledge to play any part in the process. He traces the concept of professionalism to its roots in logical positivism and the notion that scientific knowledge based on empiricism can provide prescriptions for action. In reality, the professionals he observes are engaging in a process of 'reflective conversation with the situation', which he explains as 'reflection-in-action . . . the artful inquiry by which they sometimes deal with situations of uncertainty, instability, and uniqueness' (1983, p. 268).

Schon does not take teaching as an example in his book, but his analysis of the process he observes in other professionals exactly describes what happens in classrooms. Teachers constantly exercise judgment in the light of their analysis of the situation. They hold a number of variables in their minds at one time and are capable of analyzing complex situations. They negotiate and interact with their students. Building on Schon's work one can conclude that what causes the stress for many teachers is the mismatch between their actual behaviour and the concept of professionalism they use as a model. They engage in compromise and negotiation and do not recognize them as the hallmarks of their skill but see them instead as aberrations which must be screened in a cloak of secrecy.

So, in order to build successful relationships to enable collaboration between support/advisory teachers and regular classroom teachers, it is necessary to change teachers' perceptions of what it means to be a professional.

It is also true that the Schon view of professionalism is very supportive to the notion of teacher development. Those who hold the logical positivist concept of a professional may resent the suggestion that they need development: as one teacher I interviewed said:

> I think I am developed sufficiently because of my professional training . . . it has set me up for adapting myself to changes as they occur . . . I'm of the old school, I believe teachers need to know enough about children and the needs of society to be able to make their own judgments. Having been a Deputy Head, having been in the forefront of modern mathematics, I have a pretty progressive attitude to most things in education.

This teacher's belief in himself as a professional precluded him from knowing that he needed to develop. His faith in previously acquired knowledge laid him open to the trap of routine described by Schon:

> As a practice becomes more repetitive and routine, and as known-in-practice becomes increasingly tacit and spontaneous, the practitioner may miss important opportunities to think about what he is doing. (1983, p. 61)

On the other hand, many teachers already recognize that personal and professional growth are inextricably linked with a willingness to change. For them, professional development can mean developing the skills of 'reflection-in-action'.

We are not starting at the beginning. A great deal has already been achieved through in-service training and professional development programmes. Many schools have begun breaking down teacher isolation, through open plan architecture, an open door policy, or the use of team-teaching. Sometimes this is easier to do in primary schools, but in secondary schools some subject departments with a substantial emphasis on practical work have been able to create their own mini open environment.

It is this general understanding of the need for teachers to work **together** which has led nationally to the appointment of a substantial number of support and advisory teachers. Now it is important that we build on experience, to provide a supportive environment in all schools so that they can develop collaborative partnerships.

Action Research as a Means of Developing Collaborative Partnerships

Action research presupposes that social interaction is highly complex and problematic. It recognizes that much human activity consists of ritualized patterns of behaviour in order to free the attention to grapple with what presents itself as problematic, hence, while we are concentrating hard on something else, we may walk or drive home, without any real consciousness of where we are or what we are doing, indeed, we may have meant to go somewhere quite different! Action research identifies in these ritualized patterns the reason for the well-documented failure of many curriculum development projects to bring about real change in teaching style or teacher behaviour. It is predominantly concerned with re-examining the minutae of social interaction and bringing about change. Teachers engaged in action research examine their practice to identify the actual (as opposed to intended) outcomes of their behaviour; and then take action to minimize the inevitable mismatch they have identified. The dynamic process of action research leads to professional development by encouraging and developing that 'reflexive conversation with the situation' which Schon (1983) identifies as fundamental to 'reflection-in-action'.

Therefore, action research provides an ideal methodology for collaboration between the regular classteacher and a support/advisory teacher. An action research approach ensures the establishment of the right conditions for building the relationship essential in order for professional development to take place. At the same time, the presence of two teachers in the same classroom opens up obvious possibilities for collaborative action research and enquiry. There is a symbiotic link.

Into Collaborative Action: How a Classteacher and Support Teacher Might Work Together

Getting started is obviously very important in building up trust. Here is one possible way. It is intended as an example of how two teachers might go about it. Ideally it should be discussed and adapted by those concerned. Initially, quite a lot of time is set aside for meetings and discussion. After a while this can be decreased. It will be necessary to strike the right balance of classroom experience and discussion, depending on individual circumstances.

(i) A preliminary meeting between the teacher and support/advisory teacher (henceforward called 'the support teacher')...getting to know each other...sorting out practicalities (which class, which days of the week, proposed curriculum, broad teaching aims). At this stage it is important to open up discussion of the nature of professionalism, barriers to change...importance of working together...For example, the support teacher might say:

> I don't see myself as an expert...I'm hoping to learn from this opportunity of working with you, and of course I hope you get something out of it too...Would you be interested in using this opportunity for us to carry out a joint investigation?...Perhaps we could look at some piece of student learning?...you can decide what aspect you would like us to look at after I've been to one of the classes.

(ii) A second meeting to discuss the nitty gritty of what the support teacher will do in the classroom. Planning the lesson together so that each partner has a role. For example, the support teacher might say:

> Do you want me to take part of the lesson?...or observe a particular group of students for you?...I'd like you to give me something definite to do so that we can talk about that together afterwards.

(iii) First visit of the support teacher to the classroom...introduced to the students as another teacher who is interested in working with them to develop their opportunities for learning.

(iv) A third meeting to discuss the lesson (totally non-judgmentally) and plan the next visit. Beginning to discuss a focus for the enquiry. To ensure that the classteacher takes a crucial role here the support teacher might say:

> I'm concerned that you decide what we should look at because I don't yet know the problems these students experience or what issues would interest you . . .

As suggested above, it is important that the classteacher, not the support teacher, decides on the focus of the enquiry. Here are some possibilities:

(i) One particular student's actions, words, writing and general experience of the lesson;

(ii) The differences in the learning experiences for boys and girls (or students of different ethnic or class groups);

(iii) An analysis of the skills students need/use in the lesson;

(iv) Communications in the classroom (e.g., Who contributes orally? Do the seating patterns affect participation? How do the students respond to 'open' questions as compared with 'closed' questions?);

(v) Group work and cooperation between students (possibly in relation to one particular group);

(vi) Demands made on the teacher.

The first phase of the action research will be information gathering (in research terminology, data-gathering). Once again, the classteacher, not the support teacher, should decide what methods of data-collection to use. It may be useful to collect more than one type of data so that it can be cross-checked, but it is not a good idea to collect too much data because that will be time consuming and the data will take too long to analyze. The following is a range of possibilities:

(i) A ten minute observation period, taking notes (during which time all responsibility for teaching will be taken by the other partner);

(ii) Interviews with students (either alone, in pairs, or in a group . . . probably lasting between ten minutes and half an hour);

(iii) Detailed analysis of a student's written work from photocopies;

(iv) A video recording of a lesson (to act as a focus for discussion later . . . between the two teachers . . . or involving the students . . . or with parents);

(v) An audio tape recording (to be played back several times and then short extracts of particular interest transcribed to act as a focus for discussion);

(vi) A series of photographs (to be used in a similar way to the video film).

Continuing Action: Issues of Collaborative Partnership

Who Controls the Research?

Primarily it is the classteacher who is carrying out and controlling the research with the support teacher acting as facilitator. This is a model of support which gives the teacher responsibility for his or her own learning, thus ensuring that in-service training closely matches need. It is supportive to the professionalism of the teacher, and does *not* assume there is any deficit in performance to be corrected. It presupposes Schon's model of professionalism: that is, that the hallmark of professionalism is to be a reflective practitioner, self-questioning and open to change based on analysis of situations and interactions.

The classteacher

Controlling the research is likely to mean the following:

   (i) Deciding on the focus for the investigation;
  (ii) Deciding on the methods of data-collection to be used;
 (iii) Controlling the amount of time spent on the investigation;
 (iv) Controlling others' access to the data (including a right of total veto on access);
  (v) Playing the major role in analysis of data (accepting and rejecting theories as well as sharing in their development);
 (vi) Taking decisions on action steps (changes in teaching methods, classroom organization, the learning environment, etc.);
 (vii) Planning data-collection to evaluate the results of action steps;
(viii) Deciding on any possible dissemination of findings (through informal discussions, giving talks at meetings, writing reports, etc.).

The support teacher

Facilitating the research is likely to mean the following:

(i) Participating fully in discussions with the teacher using descriptive, non-judgmental language: responding honestly but tentatively to requests for opinions;

(ii) Clarifying the action-research process for the teacher;

(iii) Agreeing with the teacher a Code of Confidentiality for the conduct of the research, ensuring the rights of participants (both teacher and students) to withhold data;

(iv) Making open suggestions for the conduct of the enquiry, being prepared to accept the teacher's final decision;

(v) Taking responsibility for teaching when asked to do so;

(vi) Collecting data when asked to do so;

(vii) Spending time on preparation of data (including some transcribing), marking of books or preparation of lessons, to ensure that the research does not constitute too great an extra burden on the teacher;

(viii) Occasionally, providing information from other research to inject new ideas (but *not* shortcircuiting the learning process by an unhelpful stress on received wisdom);

(ix) In analysis, feeding in ideas as appropriate but with an open mind;

(x) If requested, assisting with writing an account of the enquiry.

A Code of Confidentiality: Why is it Needed and What Might it Look Like?

It is important that both members of the partnership agree on ground rules to govern access to the information they gather. Even for teachers used to working with colleagues and other adults in the room there may be a certain degree of threat in engaging in a collaborative investigation. At the other extreme, some teachers may view the advent of a support teacher as part of a process of assessment or appraisal, and, without a formally stated Code of Confidentiality it may be impossible to establish a supportive relationship. Because action research is concerned with identifying problematic areas where change may improve the opportunities for learning (which is *not* the same as areas of teacher failure), this Code of Confidentiality becomes essential to set the scene for open and honest debate between the partners.

A Code of Confidentiality may look like this:

(i) Both partners will regard any notes, photographs or other material gathered during the investigation as confidential and no one else will have access to them without the agreement of both partners.

(ii) Neither partner will 'chat' casually to others about the investigation, either in the staff room or elsewhere.

(iii) If students are interviewed they will be asked for their permission before their opinions and comments are repeated to anyone else (including the other member of the partnership).

(iv) Students will be presented anonymously in any written report or presentation of research findings.

(v) Neither partner will write a report or give a talk about the investigation without fully consulting the other about what to include. Both partners have the right to veto dissemination of the research findings to anyone else.

Agreeing How Much Time it Will Take

Action research is a process. Teachers can engage in action research on any scale from very small to very extensive. One of the most important features of action research is that it begins with fact finding about the current situation and engages with issues arising out of normal day-to-day teaching. Action research is fundamentally research into the process of change so it is bound to have an effect on the classroom, but, as far as possible, it is intended to be research into a normal, undisturbed situation. It becomes counterproductive if it seriously disrupts teaching and learning by placing too great an extra burden of work on the teachers concerned. In deciding on the scale a lot depends on the resources available in terms of support teacher time, non-teaching periods, secretarial back-up, availability of tape-recorders, video-recorders, cameras and photo-copiers.

The best approach is not to decide in advance on the scale of the whole investigation, but instead to employ the concept of **bound time** at each stage (based on Len Almond's notion of **containable time**, see Almond, 1982). Bound time is fixed in advance by the partners and to make it work they have to stick to the time limits agreed. Each time slot is normally relatively short, though more time can be allowed when an activity (e.g., a session planning a lesson) would have happened anyway regardless of the research. Over two weeks it might work like this:

   (i) Half an hour is spent with the partners discussing the forthcoming lesson and planning;

  (ii) Fifteen minutes is set aside for a classroom observation, including making notes; at the same time a fifteen minute tape-recording is made of the conversation of a group of students working together;

 (iii) Half an hour is spent on listening to the tape-recording twice, making some further notes on the second time through (including noting the number counter reading at interesting points);

 (iv) Half an hour is spent with the partners discussing the notes, listening to key passages from the tape-recording and putting forward suggestions for action steps;

  (v) Action steps are planned as part of the normal process of planning another lesson;

 (vi) Half an hour is set aside for two fifteen-minute interviews with students to collect their perceptions following the action steps . . . handwritten notes are made during the interviews;

(vii) Half an hour is spent with the partners discussing the interview notes and planning further action steps.

Sharing Findings with Other Colleagues

Action research is undertaken first and foremost for the professional development of the partners. It can stop there, but if it does it might be a pity. Action research is fundamentally a collaborative process. It is grounded in the expectation that there will be free and open discussion of problematic issues between professionals. Its methods emphasize equal rights for all participants in a non-judgmental, problem-solving environment. Where possible, therefore, the original partnership will be strengthened by sharing its findings with other colleagues. New partnerships may be set up with possibilities for trying out each others' ideas.

Beyond close colleagues, too, there is much to be gained from publishing research findings. In enunciating the crucial role which teachers must play in curriculum development, Lawrence Stenhouse (1975, p. 157) wrote of the need for teachers to publish their work:

Each classroom should not be an island. Teachers working in such a tradition need to communicate with one another . . . If teachers report their own work in such a tradition, case studies will

accumulate... Professional research workers will have to master
this material and scrutinize it...

If teachers' research is not published, its circulation will be limited and it can
play no part in influencing decision-making in education. This not only
means that teachers are disempowered, but also, more seriously, deprives
decision-makers of vital knowledge from the teachers' perspective. Often
there will be opportunities for teachers to publish research papers through
their education authority or a local college or university. Alternatively, the
Classroom Action Research Network[5] holds conferences and publishes
regular Bulletins, thus providing two separate channels for disseminating
teacher research.

The Outcomes of Action Research: Professional Development in a Collaborative Partnership

Action research is a **process** and it has a variety of kinds of outcomes. First, it
is advocated here partly as a means of establishing a collaborative partnership
between a support teacher and a classteacher: if you like, as a device for
encouraging in-depth professional dialogue concerning issues of teaching
and learning. Because of its emphasis on collecting evidence it encourages
honest engagement with real issues and discourages generalizations based on
unthinking assumptions. Through its emphasis on confidentiality it also
encourages an equal partnership and dispels anxieties about a hidden
agenda of assessment or appraisal.

A second outcome of action research is in the changed relationship it
often brings between teachers and students. The process of interviewing
students increases their awareness of themselves as learners and may shift the
balance of responsibility for learning a little more towards them and away
from the teacher. This, in turn, may reduce the need for the teacher to
exercise authority over the students (though it will obviously not take it away
altogether).

Other outcomes, as already indicated, may come in terms of products
such as research reports or in-service sessions for colleagues.

Finally, there are the outcomes of professional development for the
teacher partners and improved learning opportunities for their students. If
action research is successful it should give teachers new insights into the
process of teaching. For many teachers this is profoundly exciting: it provides
a new meaning for their work as they begin to understand the complexity of
the teaching–learning process to which they are devoting a great deal of their

professional lives. To give an idea of the kinds of insights which may occur, three examples are given from the work of a group of teachers all from one school. If any of these seem obvious it should be borne in mind that there is nearly always a gap between what we intend to happen in our classrooms and what actually occurs; and it is the false assumption that this is *not* the case which stands more than anything else in the way of professional development.

Example 1

In a French lesson, the students responded well to questions in English but poorly in French. The observer/partner noted, '. . . almost every student who attempted an answer in French did so without engaging the eye of the teacher. They appeared to look at their peers, either for assistance or out of a sense of shyness.' Initially, the teacher assumed that the poor response was due to lack of knowledge of French, but in the end it proved to be equally a matter of embarrassment at speaking a foreign language in front of the teacher and/or peers. As a result of this new analysis the teacher decided not to decrease the level of difficulty for the students, but to increase the opportunities for speaking French in small groups rather than in front of the whole class.

Example 2

Some boys were getting more attention, partly through needing disciplining, but in one case through moving to the teacher and 'fetching' him. The teacher was able to ensure that he, not the boys, controlled his time in the future. The seating, which was ad hoc, allowed some difficult students to get in a position to 'survey' the whole class. The teacher rearranged the seating to prevent this and found there was less need to exercise control.

Example 3

The school had a policy to encourage active learning. In an English lesson which demanded talk and group work from students, and thinking, and cooperation while being **active**, there was quite a lot of noise and the teacher had to 'warn' the students on three or four occasions. By interviewing colleagues it emerged that, despite the policy, this kind of lesson was unusual in the school, so that students were unused to controlling their own involvement and the teacher had to hold the tension of encouraging talk/involvement/interest while aware the 'noise' was frowned upon by colleagues. In subsequent discussion with colleagues it was possible to begin to come to terms with the inevitability of increased 'noise' when moving to an active learning policy.

Notes

1 The Ford Teaching Project (1973–75), funded by the Ford Foundation, was directed by John Elliott at the Centre for Applied Research in Education, University of East Anglia. It worked with teachers in East Anglia, investigating their use of teaching methods to encourage Discovery Learning. Publications include: Cooper, D. and Ebbutt, D. (1974) 'Participation in action research as an in-service experience', *Cambridge Journal of Education*, **4**, pp. 65—71; and Bowen, R. B., Green, L. L. J. and Pols, R. (1975) 'The Ford Project — The teacher as researcher', *British Journal of In-service Education*, **2**, pp. 35–41. A range of other publications are available from the Cambridge Institute of Education.

2 The Teacher Pupil Interaction and the Quality of Learning Project (TPQL) (1980–82), funded by the Schools Council, was directed by John Elliott at the Cambridge Institute of Education. It worked with teams of teachers investigating issues concerned with teaching for understanding. Publications include Elliott, J. and Ebbutt, D. (Eds) (1986) *Case Studies in Teaching for Understanding*, Cambridge Institute of Education; and Ebbutt, D. and Elliott, J. (Eds) (1985) *Issues in Teaching for Understanding*, Longman for SCDC.

3 The Teaching, Handling Information and Learning Project (1983–85), funded by the British Library, was led by Jack Sanger and directed by Barry MacDonald at the Centre for Applied Research in Education, University of East Anglia. Publications include Sanger, J. (Ed.) (forthcoming) *Classrooms In-formation*, British Library; and Schostak, J. (Ed.) (1988) *Breaking into the Curriculum*.

4 Pupil Autonomy in Learning with Microcomputers (PALM) (1988–90), funded by the Microelectronics Education Support Unit, is led by Bridget Somekh and directed by John Elliott at the Centre for Applied Research in Education, University of East Anglia. It is working with schools in Cambridgeshire, Essex and Norfolk, looking at the way in which

microcomputers can help to create an environment for autonomous learning.

5   The Classroom Action Research Network (CARN) was founded in 1976 by John Elliott as a means of continuing to support the work of the teachers after the end of the Ford Teaching Project. It has a steering group representing local and regional action research groups in Britain and overseas, and a coordinator, Bridget Somekh. CARN runs regular conferences and publishes annual Bulletins of action research papers which are available from CARN, at the Centre for Applied Research in Education, University of East Anglia. Purchase of CARN publications ensures your name on the mailing list.

Chapter 7

The Visible Supporter with No Invisible Means of Support:
The ESG Teacher and the Classteacher

Patrick Easen

John Buchan once described an atheist as 'a man who has no invisible means of support'. In this chapter I want to borrow that concept and suggest that many advisory and support teachers, whether from the Education Support Grant (ESG) schemes or other LEA projects, might be described as atheistic in relation to any model of teacher learning. Whilst the conscious disbelief or denial implied by such a term as atheist may be inappropriate (since many seem not to have either explicitly or systematically considered the issue of teacher learning), the implication that there may be no underlying belief system behind an important facet of their professional activity may be justified. This seems strange when the proliferation of such posts in one form or another suggests an assumption that they are an effective catalyst for change within schools. Without doubt they are a very 'visible' form of support for teachers in classrooms but it is less certain how effective they are in terms of developing practice within those classrooms.

The evidence for the effectiveness of these 'visible supporters' is thin. For example, Petrie (1988), whilst acknowledging that 'it is too early to make any definite statement about the long term success of the ESG science project on classroom practice and hence on children's learning', claims that:

> . . . it is possible to report an overwhelming acceptance of advisory teachers in the schools, and of the classroom support of the teacher. It is also possible to say categorically that advisory teachers have been instrumental in catalysing science experiences for children in many instances where one suspects that otherwise would not have occurred.

Similarly in relation to one particular ESG project, Straker (1988) asserts that:

> In their capacity as change agents, the advisory teacher had clearly made an impact on mathematics teaching in the project schools . . . This interventionist approach would only be effective, however, if long-term change were to be realised in the project schools. At this stage, one can only speculate whether this will occur. The heads and teachers were optimistic about future developments.

Such reports, of course, merely serve to emphasize the difficulty of evaluating impact upon the classroom processes of teaching and learning; an area which is a veritable minefield of methodological problems. Accepting such difficulties, it might be sufficient to suggest that, as long as these ESG (and similar) developments build upon the growing body of knowledge about working with teachers, then there should be little cause for concern. So far, however, there seems to be little to reassure me that even this is the case.

This chapter draws upon work with a range of advisory and support teachers over a period of three years. Much has been with groups of a homogeneous nature, for example, Primary Science ESG, Mathematics ESG or Learning Support teachers. Working with techniques based upon the use of images and metaphors, an attempt has been made to examine the way in which such teachers frame problems of educational innovation and change and, in the process, their own roles. Through uncovering the assumptions and definitions tacit in particular choices of role-frames it was hoped that a better understanding of the strategies employed by advisory and support teachers in their school-based work might be achieved. In parallel with this there has been some small-scale action research work involving one particular ESG teacher in relation to two primary schools. The latter has explored ways of creating awareness with individual teachers of the possibilities for change and of providing support so that change becomes possible.

Advisory/support teachers spend a large part of their time in schools and much of this is classroom-based. For example, Straker (1988) found that this constituted an average of about 40 per cent of a typical week for his sample. The phrase classroom-based work with teachers can encompass a wide variety of interpretations and practices. Although it may mean the advisory/support teacher and the classteacher working together, it may be more accurately described as working alongside or in the same teaching area at the same time. Consequently I decided to classify the various strategies discussed according to the 'control' of the children in the teaching area. Thus *total control* gave full responsibility for planning and delivering the experiences in that area to one person; *allocated control* gave spheres of

Figure 7.1 Strategies available to advisory/support teachers for working with classteachers

Type of control		Strategies for classroom-based work with teachers
1 'Total control' rests with one person	1A	The advisory/support teacher works with the class; the classteacher observes
	1B	The classteacher works with the class; the advisory/support teacher observes
2 'Allocated control' between the two	2A(i)	The advisory/support teacher works with the class; the classteacher works with an individual child
	2A(ii)	The advisory/support teacher works with the class; the classteacher works with a group of children
	2B(i)	The classteacher works with the class; the advisory/support teacher works with an individual child
	2B(ii)	The classteacher works with the class; the advisory/support teacher works with a group of children
3 'Collaborative control' between the two	3	Advisory/support teacher and classteacher work together with the class

control to each person; and *collaborative control* involved planning and working together with the whole teaching group in a form of team-teaching. This enabled me to produce a typification of the strategies used by advisory/support teachers dependent upon the degree of responsibility carried for teaching the children during classroom-based work with teachers (see Figure 7.1).

This typification seemed helpful, not only to classify current practices but also to pinpoint how thes strategies might be related to any model of teacher learning. Strategies identified both by practitioners and in the literature seemed to have evolved for historical reasons when adapted from previous practices or as ways of gaining credibility for new initiatives rather than from any coherent overview of their role in teacher development. Thus, for example, many learning support teachers make almost exclusive use of strategy 2B(i) working with individual children — because of the expectations of the host school and of the classteachers. This in itself being an outgrowth of previous perceptions of 'special needs' teaching. On the other hand, the ESG project team described by Straker appear to have used strategy 2B(ii) followed by either strategy 1A or strategy 3 — although whether this was a conscious decision is not clear:

> As a means of gaining the confidence and respect of the teachers... the project team had initially worked with small

groups of children while the class teacher taught the remainder. The acceptance of the outsider therefore developed gradually in a non-threatening manner until the team members were either taking the whole class or engaging in team teaching with the class teacher.

At this point the dilemma for the advisory/support teacher becomes clear, for their work is invariably underpinned by an implicit requirement for a significant change in teaching style in many of the classrooms in which they work. In effect, their work is often about creating new norms of practice within the host classrooms and schools. This is not an easy thing to do since all practice is nested within a matrix of assumptions about such things as the nature of knowledge, how children learn, what teaching involves and so on. It is these that teachers use to put meaning upon their experience of teaching and they represent, in total, a way of seeing the world of the classroom. What teachers *do* about learning in the classroom seems to be a function of what they *think* about learning in the classroom. 'Practice', then, only appears to be transformed when the 'meaning-perspective' itself is transformed. This view of teacher learning is one that has featured in several recent works on educational change. Consequently any working with teachers directed towards transformatory learning may involve helping the classteacher to:

- Explore, clarify and 'make sense' of existing practices and value systems (otherwise the limitations of these may not be realized);
- Replace the set of understandings or meanings which underpin existing practices with a new set of understandings or meanings which can guide the development of new practices; and
- Try out and become confident in new practices (and the concomitant value systems).

Such a view helps to clarify *what* strategies may be the most productive for an advisory/support teacher to use with a classteacher and *when*, in the process of developing practice, some strategies become appropriate. Furthermore, it also indicates the limitations of other strategies.

Reviewing the strategies typified in Figure 7.1 it seems reasonable to suggest that both of those identified as type 1 have limited value. Strategy 1A, although common practice, casts the advisory/support teacher in the role of 'expert'. As Davies and Davies (1988) point out this may be 'a seductive mystique to perpetuate' but carries the danger of de-skilling the classteacher. Both de Boo (1988), who calls it 'teaching demonstrations' and Straker (1988), who uses the term 'clinical model', see value in this strategy.

The former because 'the teachers began to value the opportunity to observe and discuss the ESG teacher's approach and questioning technique'; the latter because 'teachers saw the value of group work, practical and investigative approaches and began to appreciate the need for children to engage in mathematical discussion'. Whilst not denying the validity of their comments, the strategy does raise issues of interpersonal sensitivity and demands both careful planning of what the classteacher does whilst the strategy is employed (observing an individual child, noting types of response and so on) and thorough debriefing afterwards. In the absence of such conditions neither the practices themselves nor the intentions underpinning them may be clearly understood. More worryingly, if there are grave dangers of creating dependency for the classteacher then, by requiring the advisory/support teacher to wear the expert's mantle, there is the greater danger of the latter ceasing to be open to new learning or any 'risk-taking' in the classroom.

Strategy 1B, although offering potential for evaluating practice, is the sort of thing that tends only to contribute to the development of practice through the sensitive but rigorous debriefing available within the robust relationship of 'critical friendships'. These take time to develop and, in the case of the ESG teacher involved in the action research, after nearly 18 months was achieved only with the subject coordinator in one school who:

> agreed to video each other working with children and . . . view this together on a regular basis. [field notes]

The strategies identified as type 2A can be seen as having very clear purposes. Strategies 2A(i) and 2A(ii) offer the potential for the classteacher to engage in either close observation of pupil experience (and thus explore existing practices and beliefs) or experimentation with new practice (and thus gain confidence in it). For example, the ESG teacher in the action research explored successfully both strategy 2A(i) when

> . . . it is possible . . . [for a teacher] . . . to sit with a group of children, observing closely one or two of the group

and strategy 2A(ii) when

> . . . staff undertook to use the [Dime] material with some children, and to report back . . . this meant working with the rest of the class to enable the teacher to work with a group. [field notes]

In order for such purposes to be achieved the advisory/support teacher needs to spend time beyond the classroom contact doing things such as analyzing the observation with the teacher or helping with the planning of something that the teacher wants to try (including helping to identify clear criteria for success) and then debriefing the work.

Type 2B strategies offer the opportunity to indicate to the classteacher the potential for pupil learning of some piece of new practice. It is not unusual for teachers to be sceptical of the practicality or worthwhileness of new ideas if they have never experienced them. The problem, then, is how to give sufficient insight into new practices so that disbelief may be suspended and a window of opportunity created for the new practice to begin growing in the classroom. This is not an easy thing to do for these strategies run the danger of the advisory/support teacher being seen as the 'expert' who can perform in ways that the 'ordinary, overpressed classteacher' cannot — a syndrome referred to by Lofthouse (1987) as the 'travelling salesman, with a few magic tricks thrown in'. For these strategies to really work the advisory/support teacher needs both considerable sensitivity in acknowledging the existing skills, efforts and provision of the classteacher and a structured way of feeding back the outcomes of these strategies into the teacher's development. The ESG teacher involved in the action research, for example, noted:

> ... Whilst working with groups of children, in a situation in which it was difficult for the teacher to observe closely what was happening I wrote an account of each session in order to report back. Although this in itself did not enable first hand observation, it provided a mechanism for sharing experience ... [field notes]

The final strategy reviewed, type 3, through its opportunity for enabling the advisory/support teacher and the classteacher to construct shared understandings or meanings about practice (both existing and new) seems to offer the potential of some of the other strategies discussed within an atmosphere described by Davies and Davies (1988) as, ' ... of *positive professional exchange* through which mutual support and respect can be fostered'.

In terms of both 'the change process' and ways of 'helping' class-teachers this strategy would seem to be the most complete. It involves no pre-conceived assumptions about the 'needs' of that particular classroom (for these are identified and articulated during the work) and accepts that it is up to the classteacher to evolve workable ways of developing practice (albeit with the support of another experienced teacher). It can be a satisfying professional experience for the advisory/support teacher:

> ... after a session of working with ... [a teacher] ... I realized how relaxed I felt when working with her and her children. We do

discuss our perceptions after each session and plan the details of where to next based on a longer term plan previously formulated (but flexible and constantly re-evaluated). The emphasis is on joint planning and dividing and interchanging responsi-bilities . . . . [field notes]

Shared meaning *can* be built upon shared experiences if the advis-ory/support teacher realizes the importance of this and takes active steps to ensure it. This might involve building a professionally respectful but enquiring relationship with the classteacher and negotiating an arrangement for joint planning and evaluating of the shared teaching. De Boo (1988) noted that, 'The teachers showed a preference for team-teaching' (i.e., this particular strategy) but then went on to comment, 'The drawback here is that time has to be found to share and discuss the development later (not always possible).'

It is, however, difficult to understand how any of the classroom-based work can make sense without such a requirement (as has been noted already). This then, takes us back to the point that such work needs to be underpinned by some view of how teachers learn. Figure 7.2 summarizes the previous discussion and pinpoints some of the possible implications for advisory/support teachers when using these strategies. Even with an awareness of those implications some strategies might be considered more 'high risk' than others; without that awareness the longer term effectiveness of any classroom-based work is problematic.

Figure 7.2 The potential of various strategies for classroom-based work and possible implications for the advisory/support teacher

Strategy for classroom-based work	Potential for helping teachers to develop practice	Possible requirements for the strategy to be effective
A: Advisory/support teacher works with class; classteacher observes	Enables demonstration of new practice by advisory/support teacher	• Interpersonal sensitivity on part of advisory/support teacher • Careful planning of what the classteacher does during the session • Thorough debriefing
B: Classteacher works with class; advisory/support teacher observes	Enables evaluation of practice	• Building of 'critical friendship' • Sensitive but rigorous debriefing

Figure 7.2 Continued

Strategy for classroom-based work	Potential for helping teachers to develop practice	Possible requirements for the strategy to be effective
A(i) and (ii): Advisory/ support teacher works with class; classteacher works with individual or group	● Enables close observation of pupil experience (for both existing and new practice)	● Negotiation of who/what/how of the observation ● Collaborative analysis of the observation and debriefing
	● Enables experimentation by classteacher with new practice	● Joint planning for implementation to ensure success ● Clarification of 'classroom indicators' for success in the new practice ● Thorough debriefing
2 B(i) and (ii): Classteacher works with class; advisory/support teacher works with individual or group	● Enables advisory/support teacher to indicate potential for pupil learning of new practice	● Sensitivity on part of advisory/support teacher in acknowledging existing skills, efforts and provision of classteacher ● Structured way of feeding back the outcomes of these strategies into teacher development
3 Advisory/support teacher and classteacher work together in the class	● Enables construction of shared understanding or meanings about practice (either existing or new)	● Negotiating a regular cycle of collaborative planning, action and reflection with the classteacher ● Acknowledging, respecting and responding to the practices and perspectives of the classteacher

Finally, I have examined only the strategies used when working with individual teachers. As was stated earlier, this is usually concerned with creating new forms of practice. However, in order for new practice to be sustained the advisory/support teacher needs to address not only the individual teacher in his or her classroom but also the wider school context. This may involve creating new structures to support these practices and building the professional culture of the school. In other words, the problems of helping individual teachers learn and develop their classroom practice are nested within the problems of helping teachers collectively to learn and develop their practice. Success, then, will not be merely a matter of the quantity or even the quality of the visible support made available to a school, but may well be a function of the quality of the 'invisible means of support'!

Managing a Support Service

Chapter 8

Supporting a Teaching Support Service: Curriculum Change Through Action Research

Maggie McKenna

Context

What follows is an account of the means by which one LEA's Teaching Support Service and some of its mainstream schools have worked collaboratively to stimulate curriculum development initiatives with particular reference to the special educational needs (SEN) of pupils.[1]

The Teaching Support Service consists of a team of peripatetic teachers serving the Metropolitan Borough as a direct teaching and advisory service in 148 schools. It has been developed over a ten year period to respond to the needs of children identified by the Authority's 7+ screening procedure. From a core of fifteen staff initially, it now has a compliment of fifty-seven full-time teaching staff including: Head and Deputy of Service, and nine Area/Curriculum Leader posts. A change of name from Remedial Service in 1987 did not necessarily mean a changed perception or role either within the service or within schools.

The service operated a traditional small-group withdrawal system and staff recruitment was based on this description of role. The service had always sustained a programme of in-service training aimed at skilling teachers to fulfill the traditional remedial concept of support.

In recent years there has been a need to re-examine the concept of 'support' and the styles being operated in the light of policy-led research, changing educational objectives and new forms of operation from interest groups and HMI. Additionally, growing awareness within the support service and schools of the possible inappropriateness and inefficiency of the support styles being operated has created pressure to examine and reconceptualize the role.

The existing model of support thus required confronting the traditional perceptions both within the service and within schools. A process of unfreezing was therefore vital in order to create a climate in which change could be effected. Although no formal mandate for change was offered at LEA level, interest and support was forthcoming from individual members of the service.

Why and How to Change

The pressures identified earlier, arising from both a national context and perceived local needs, created a climate in which it became necessary to review and, if possible, reconceptualize the role of the visiting support teacher within mainstream schools. Senior personnel in both schools and the support service were questioning the effectiveness of the current model of relationships based on the withdrawal of children, identified as having special needs in literacy and/or mathematics, in small groups or one-to-one situations. Accordingly, a small-scale enquiry was initiated to collect the perceptions of staff in nine schools covering the 5–13 age range and those of a selected cross-section of support teachers representing different areas of expertise and levels of responsibility. Information was gathered by involving this core group (who demonstrated an active interest and willingness to invest time) in an examination of their own role in school. Data was generated under two general, but overlapping, headings.

— The advantages and disadvantages of their own present style of operation.
— The strengths and weaknesses of the support currently offered to schools generally.

As a result of this exercise, key issues were perceived to be:

The Teaching Process

School and classroom management.
Styles of teaching.
Teacher attitude and expectation.
Teacher awareness.
Teacher training/in-service.
Inappropriate curriculum.
Stereotyping — of children/teachers involved in SEN work.
Involvement of subject specialists.
Mixed-ability teaching.
Status of SEN within the school.
Communication.

Collaborative Issues

Identification of requirements of collaborative teaching.
In-service to develop relevant skills.
Will change be enforced?
Time to talk.
Sharing responsibilities — resourcing, planning, teaching.
Ownership of the initiative.
Flexibility of model for change.
Cross-curricular dimension.
Relationships.
Communication.
Evaluation.
Negotiation.

The generated issues provided pre-conditions for developing collaborative styles of support.

Impetus was added to this activity in so far as the 1981 Education Act had now been effectively implemented within the LEA and thereby schools were legally required to respond appropriately to pupils with SEN. At the same time, since staffing ratios within schools had fallen, there was less specialist 'remedial' help available. The local environment was conducive, therefore, to an examination of how the support time which was available might be deployed to the greater benefit of pupils, individual teachers and whole schools. Encouragingly, there was also a recognition that whole-school engagement with devising strategies for SEN, although not identified explicitly as in-service training, could nevertheless contribute to the professional development of school staff.

Whilst enthusiastic for a general re-shaping and redirection of activity, senior personnel in the support service recognized that managing such an undertaking on a large-scale basis would be problematic in terms of preparing staff for the change. It was decided that the majority of the service, for the time being, would continue in the style already functioning i.e., withdrawal, or 'in-class' support for individual children. In parallel, however, the support service developed a group of its own staff who were personally competent, confident and committed to working in a collab-orative style with their school-based colleagues. Such a group already existed in embryo and what now had to be done was to provide a springboard for its development such that members might subsequently spearhead the changes envisaged.

Collaboration as a Key Concept

One of the first tasks confronting the core group of support teachers was to clarify its own understandings of what collaboration meant in practice, who might be involved and what forms of preparation, planning and maintenance it might require to be successful. Collaboration was seen as both a value and a strategy. It was a mode of working which acknowledged the personal and professional worth of the parties involved and which used their expertise to achieve mutually agreed objectives through partnership, authentic dialogue and a commitment to plan, act and evaluate jointly. In Lieberman's (1986) words, it resides essentially in 'working with, not working on' and as a process it initially entails systematic and sensitive communication in order to:

— Establish trust and professional credibility.
— Identify a set of clear and shared objectives.
— Clarify roles amongst the participants.
— Generate a sense of ownership and responsibility for the project.

To an outsider, the task of clarifying a key concept may appear a misuse of support teachers' time, if not a little pedantic. Yet our experience leads us to believe there is value in the process. Organizational change is a lengthy business and results are slow. If the core group were unclear about the values and processes central to a reconceptualized role this would affect subsequent action and could prejudice progress.

Action Research as a Key Process

The strategy chosen by the support service to bring about change was derived from a model of organizational development taken up by educationalists in this country as a means of promoting change and improving practice. The aim of the strategy is 'to utilise information to collaborate in a problem-solving process which will improve professional functioning'. This process is known as action research and its implication for schools is that teachers themselves will become researchers into their own practice and will, thereby, own and control their own professional development (Stenhouse, 1975). Although it differs fundamentally from other research paradigms, action research is nevertheless a structured and consciously reflective approach involving a managed progression through a cycle of interrelated processes. These can be represented diagrammatically as follows (Figure 8.1):

Figure 8.1 The action research cycle

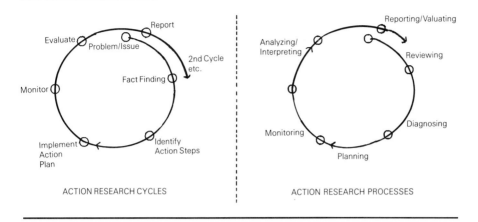

ACTION RESEARCH CYCLES | ACTION RESEARCH PROCESSES

(Bell and Pennington, 1988)

The group of support teachers participating in this enterprise used an action-research approach to examine how collaboration might be established in practice and what strategy might best facilitate the management of this process. The suggested Action Phases that emerged are represented in Figure 8.2 (p. 102).

Serious and managed engagement with such developments is time consuming and entails a great deal of negotiation to clarify meanings, processes and anticipated outcomes. Investing time at this preliminary stage is, however, worthwhile both in terms of ownership and future effectiveness. Whilst 'prophets may teach private wisdom; teachers must deal in public knowledge' (Stenhouse, 1975). Establishing public knowledge and making private understandings explicit is a key objective of these interactive, collaborative endeavours. Worthwhileness for all parties involved depends on committing resources to these fundamental activities. Given the potential of this model for effecting change, additional support strategies were provided for participants. The focus was on research methodology and project management training, complemented by periodic access to an external consultant. It is essential that the style of INSET provision reflects the values and processes of the collaborative projects themselves in that they are highly interactive, problem oriented and collegial. 'We emphasised that all participants would be vital members of the group valued as much for their support as for their talents, ideas and participations' (Paquette, 1987).

Figure 8.2 Outline project management strategy

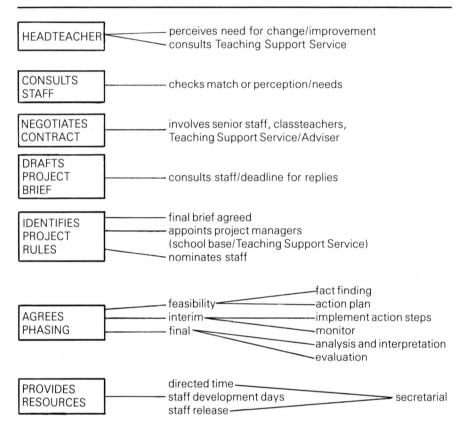

Model of the Process

Initial dialogue about possible new styles of operation were often initiated *informally*, either by staff from within the schools or by support service staff. Interest in collaborative work was frequently aroused through in-service provision and knowledge of other collaborative ventures. In addition, the raised awareness of the needs of children generated a desire to provide appropriate responses. Acting on informal approaches was relatively easy as the support service already had a presence in most schools, the extent of this being determined by the number of identified children within the institution. Thus, whilst negotiating access to the schools was not problematic, it was more difficult to establish an alternative style of support as this required both collaborating institutions to develop some form of 'contract'. It required a set of explicit and mutually agreed procedures. The processes involved in the establishment of such a 'contract' can be illustrated through the following five step framework:

Confront	— identifying and explicitly owning the issue.
Understand	— sharing the problem — clear and unambiguous communication.
Define	— aiming at mutually acceptable definitions of the problem or issue area.
Search	— collaborative exploration of ways in which available joint resources can be best utilized and exploited.
Agree	— to undertake a school-based project using an action-research mode with agreed definition of style and duration.

Using such a framework may appear somewhat mechanistic, but it has the merits of guiding activity in the initial stages of *contract building* and experience has shown that a professionally beneficial relationship between the school and the support service can be established through such a structured approach. Moreover it has the clear adantage of making explicit to both parties their **joint** agreements about objectives, desired outcomes, rights, obligations and resource usage (including the thorny issue of finite time).

The presence of a contract provides credibility for all participants when they have to report back to their host institutions and peers, and it creates a situation in which all individuals are informed. At a personal level these individuals come out of the process with improved confidence, a sense of personal worth, more control and a mandate for change. More importantly they know they are going to operate in a mutually supportive environment. In a very real sense, building the contract can become transformational and Vanderslice (1983) captures the essence of this when he says:

> As a result of these changed perceptions and increased skills, combined with joining others to take a group action, people begin to act more powerfully by taking more control and responsibility in all levels of their social world.

An example of one such contract negotiated with a school can be seen in Appendix I (pp. 115–17 of this volume).

Starting the Initiative

A degree of conscious matching of school with support teachers has been an essential element of progress thus far and a period of preparation is also required so that support teachers may develop adequate skills for working in a collaborative style. Care has to be taken during these initial stages that expectations are not excited which cannot be subsequently resourced. As information about collaborative projects percolated through the LEA's informal communication network, the support service had to avoid finding itself in the potentially embarrassing situation of being unable to respond to all requests for collaborative curriculum development. For this reason no explicit 'marketing' of such initiatives was undertaken.

It was also felt to be important that flexibility of response to particular contexts was retained and that different forms of response could well operate **within** an individual school. It was always recognized that new modes of operation would exist **alongside** and be **integrated with** existing modes. It was therefore essential that practical decisions were agreed regarding such issues as:

— Targeted curriculum areas/year group/staff.
— Deployment of support time.
— Timetabling to facilitate effective collaboration (teaching *and* regular meeting times).
— Responsibility for those identified children within the school no longer receiving direct support teaching.

Once these general, but fundamental, issues were dealt with, it was imperative to examine closely how the approach should/could be promoted both with the identified school group (normally targeted by the head-teachers) but also with the staff as a whole. This was crucial if the initiative was to be a whole-school development, intended to effect structured (deep) rather than peripheral (surface) change.

The involvement of subject coordinators across the schools, whether committed to a direct teaching role within the project or not, was planned as a device to encourage and facilitate effective curriculum development. Inadequate briefing of the whole staff at this juncture could potentially create conflict and tension as the project ensued, which was, indeed, the case in one instance.

Taking time to establish common understanding, intended outcomes, the rationale behind them, the choice of a targeted group/subject and the opportunties for staff response to the proposals is increasingly seen as an important ingredient to subsequent success. If such collaborative work is intended to facilitate whole-school and whole staff professional development, it must not risk undermining or failure as a result of inadequate planning, informing and discussion. This cannot be overemphasized.

How Projects are Activated

'Contracts' can act initially as a 'working brief' or 'discussion paper' for the group which is to collaborate. The suggested time scale by the support service for planning such work is a term prior to the commencement of collaborative teaching and, when possible, a weekly meeting is held throughout the term. Although this may seen generous (and time for such meetings is generally managed by headteachers through timetable manipulation), it has been shown repeatedly that the ground covered during this phase is crucial. It has much less to do with teaching, as such, than with the sensitive issue of establishing a workable and meaningful group relationship. Typical issues examined during this initial period of group formation (Tuckman, 1965) are:

— Identifying, sharing and agreeing aims and objectives of the collaborative ventures.
— Clarifying the group task through recognition of the differences between the present situation and the preferred target.
— Role clarification for individuals, negotiated through their own and others' perceptions of strengths and preferences.
— Addressing individuals' concerns in terms of interpretations of 'collaboration', i.e. agreeing a definition in **practical** terms.
— Clarifying the institution's expectations of the group.
— Agenda setting, both for individuals *and* the group.

Also, importantly, a point made by Lewis (1985):

The principle that the day-to-day reality of accomplishing tasks effectively and efficiently would be seen in the context of the numerous other demands of the daily life of a school.

The importance of the issue described above must not be minimized since the classteacher may initially perceive the collaborative endeavour as something above and beyond existing demands, rather than as an opportunity to develop both personally and professionally through working with other colleagues in an alternative style.

Action research, by definition, is a process of learning, effected through engaging in certain activities; it is therefore only to be expected that teachers may, *initially*, be unaware of the personal and professional benefits to them as individuals, as well as the benefits to the whole school which can be realized through such engagement. Collaborating colleagues together travel along avenues which lead them to a recognition of the opportunities presented through researching practice:

Action Research — aims to feed practical judgement in concrete situations, and the validity of the 'theories' it generates depend not so much on 'scientific' tests of truth, as on their usefulness in helping people to act more intelligently and skilfully. In action research, 'theories' are not validated and then applied to practice. They are validated through practice. (Elliott, 1983)

Importance of Role Clarification

Role is the behaviour we generate as a result of a set of expectations. Once shared aims and objectives for projects are agreed by the group, it is essential that individual members are aware of:

(a) expectations (from school/support service management) as these relate to their particular responsibilities within the institution; and

(b) the participative responsibilities they have **within** the project group framework.

It is our experience that in situations where obligatory, directive and voluntary participative elements coexist, the possibility of role conflict, role overload and role ambiguity abound. For this reason, it is important to spend time clarifying key roles within the project framework and to consider their relationship to participants' existing roles and duties. The benefits of undertaking such a role clarification exercise before starting a project are that:

— possible mismatch of expectations is avoided;
— a framework within which to function is created;
— professional identity is established and recognized by colleagues;
— each individual is a valued group member;
— the targeting of specific areas for developmental thinking and planning is facilitated;
— a sense of commitment is encouraged which generates ownership.

Where the individual's role is clear within the institution's functioning and where it correlates with personal/group self-interest, change can be effective. Making role relationships and expectations explicit, defining responsibilities, establishing time frames and the focus of control/ownership therefore provides participants with shared understanding and interpretations, conducive to growth and supported development.

Role of Project Coordinators/Managers/Facilitators

In the context of the kinds of projects being described here, is a clearly identified need for key personnel to act as 'coordinators' of intergroup processes, 'managers' of resources and 'facilitators' of on-going activity. In the model employed by the support service, engagement with these tasks occurs at two levels: 'insider' facilitators and 'outsider' consultants.

'Insider' Facilitators are commissioned by the support service to manage the development of a project. Each has a specific, but interrelated brief, in terms of what the project group expects of him/her with regard to practical outcomes. Each is also required to provide support in the broadest sense, both to motivate staff *and* to sustain the project within a whole school context with a view to effecting long-term change. If facilitators are to be effective in realizing these twin objectives, it has been shown within the projects that they require a recognized status within the institution. However, that alone would be an unsatisfactory criterion by which to identify such personnel. Of more significance are credibility, both within the peer group and with the senior management of the school and the support service. They need good interpersonal skills; access to decision-making and policy-formation bodies and the capacity to be involved and committed, but at the same time they need to retain a certain distance so that a more global view of issues can be offered.

If these abilities aggregate within facilitators they can engage with the sponsorship, advocacy and legitimation of activities necessary for maintaining a creative tension between exerting pressure (as part of the management team) and providing support (as part of the group) to keep the project moving forwards. A crucial factor, of course, to the effective execution of this role is the ability to communicate at a number of different levels, so that agreed interpretations are transmitted in an undistorted form between all the interests involved.

The insider facilitator's role then, is essentially one of managing a project team of peer professionals. Davies *et al*. (1988) have identified nine major elements in this task and their framework (see Figure 8.3) provides a useful means of describing the managerial content of this role.

'Outsider' Consultants are used to provide in-service education and training for a core of support teachers so that they may develop greater knowledge of their own practice with a view to developing collaborative projects. The central purpose of this support service initiated programme of INSET was to examine issues associated with managing a change of support style from one in which the teachers worked in isolation to one which was collaborative, developmental and based on classroom teachers taking charge of their own context-specific professional development.

Figure 8.3 Managerial content of the facilitator's role

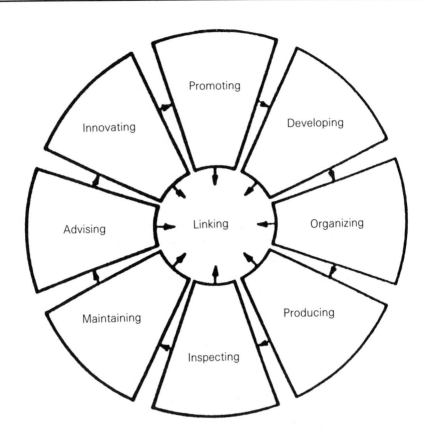

Innovating	– Creating and experimenting with new approaches to work
Promoting	– Searching for and persuading others of new approaches
Developing	– Assessing the viability and applicability of new approaches
Organizing	– Establishing and implementing ways and means of making things work
Producing	– Progressing and completing task outputs on a regular basis
Inspecting	– Checking and auditing systems to ensure they are working to high standards
Maintaining	– Ensuring that principles, processes and standards are maintained within the working group
Advising	– Gathering and sharing the necessary information and resources
Linking	– Managing and coordinating the work of the team and its members in the above functions to achieve the objectives.

Davis *et al.* (1988)

Developing Support Teachers

A planned, coherent programme of INSET enables support teachers to engage systematically with a range of issues they had themselves identified as crucial for a shift in working style. These included: role clarification exercises, the development of negotiating skills, means of promoting ownership of projects, rehearsal of interpersonal and group interaction skills and strategies for managing change at personal, group and organizational levels.

A second element in the INSET programme was to encourage the group to examine ways in which action research might support their activities in primary and middle schools. Through such an approach, collaborative fact finding, action planning, monitoring of action steps, interpreting and evaluating data, and reporting outcomes of efforts to improve practical, professional concerns became key procedures. A further objective of this approach was to identify the strengths, weaknesses and opportunities that action research offered as a mode of collaborating with other teachers and the list generated by the group was particularly useful in suggesting practical means of engaging with factors which both helped and hindered progress towards the new mode of working.

Collaborative Professional Development

There was also a clear recognition by the support group that if collaboration was intended at project level within the schools, there were implications for collaborative professional development at in-service level. This took the form of 'pairing' those support teachers and classteachers who were already collaborating within a teaching situation to enable joint access to the external consultant. By this means, access to expertise was broadened. It was shared and a forum for professional dialogue was created in which the collaborative activities of both individuals could be mutually and collectively reviewed. 'Paired teachers' reported jointly to the group (which included some support teachers on the verge of being involved in new initiatives) under four categories:

— The content of involvement.
— Styles of collaborative teaching adopted.
— Results of collaborative action.
— Interpretations of outcomes and proposals for future action.

A substantial list of issues arose from this process. Some were very much related to individual contexts and the substantive areas of collaborative work. Of more general interest, however, were those which related to future action and means for securing greater effectiveness between the support service/support teachers and schools/collaborating classroom teachers. These included:

— increasing the emphasis on joint evaluation and assessment procedures;
— modifying and structuring resource distribution to include review and evaluation procedures;
— developing guidelines for collaborative teaching and evaluation;
— improving joint staff development strategies;
— increasing planning for support activities and active management of a wider group of staff to involve them in collaborative teaching situations.

The Role of the External Consultant and Network Building

In this context, the role of the external consultant was effective because it was 'framed in terms of process' and 'external coordination' rather than in terms of 'content' (Bell, 1985). A clear responsibility was placed upon the consultants to work in a manner which generated descriptions of practice amongst the practitioners themselves rather than employing a style of learning centred on the study of texts. This mode of operation had several advantages: the context and style were non-threatening; sensitive issues could be examined without pejorative judgments, since the outsider was professionally distanced; the consultant ensured that all issues were given adequate 'air-time'; and greater mutual understandings were facilitated by the skilful management of professional dialogue. Through the sharing of ideas, concerns and possible developments, joint ownership and a sense of partnership was reinforced. Collaboration was no longer an issue seen as focusing on the individual school's curriculum development; it became professional collaboration which could be sustained outside the perimeter of the school.

Thus, the action research cycle entered its second phase with:

— The researching of **joint** practice.
— The examination of issues collectively.
— A commitment to act on the outcomes collaboratively.

A support network was created whereby project schools were aware of each others' developments, concerns and aspirations. This was essential to sustain progress (cf. Bell and Pennington, 1988) and to ensure that collaborative activities did not become semi-detached or even isolated from the main thrust of the support service policy. In a different cultural context, Gould and Letven (1987) make the point that:

> Through alliances and networks, members help each other maintain the spirit of inquiry crucial to the healthy intellectual life of all faculty members, regardless of the age of their students.

A natural development was then to extend the network by involving the external consultant in the schools themselves. The key strategic task here is to ensure that what has already been gained is not lost. Collaboration is more firmly founded at both an institutional and system level if this group includes the headteacher, the general adviser, the participating teachers and managers from both collaborating institutions. The strengths of such a development are pronounced:

— An authority and power base is established.
— Projects become whole-school focused.
— Ownership becomes broader.
— Collaboration can now become 'vertical' as well as 'horizontal'.
— Increased familiarity with the nature of the activities by senior management generates a predisposition to further support and resource developments.
— Maintenance and progress are seen to be sponsored and supported both from within the school and from without.

Evaluation as a Key Activity

The meetings described above form a scenario for the evaluation of developments within the projects, in terms of the perceptions of all participants. Additionally, the evaluation of whole-school development is facilitated and recognized by the LEA. The creation of a forum for the dissemination of good practice can lead to advocacy and sponsorship. Evaluations are viewed as being concerned with improving performance through observation, and there is growing awareness amongst the collaborating teachers of the important issues surrounding the planning and teaching of a worthwhile curriculum rather than an obsessive involvement with subject and content.

Examples of evaluation approaches include the following:

Example 1
The group involved in the generation of this on-going evaluative procedure (completed fortnightly by all group members involved in direct teaching), was attempting new styles of curriculum delivery. The evaluations provide a springboard for discussion about developments and possible improvements/modifications to delivery styles and resourcing.

Example 2
A summative evaluation was requested by the collaborating teachers and was produced by the school's general adviser. It represented the results of periodic visits by the adviser during the year's project and a meeting of all participants (whether or not involved in direct teaching) during the final stages, at which a carefully managed dialogue, focusing on particular questions, took place.

Example 3
The group in this instance chose, as its summative evaluation, to employ the strategy of Forcefield Analysis. All members contributed both their positive and negative perceptions of the year's collaborative venture. These were collated by the school's project manager and the outcomes discussed in detail by the group at a full meeting attended by the headteacher.

All three examples are publicly meaningful and provide information which can be utilized in decision-making about further development.

> Action learning particularly obliges subjects to become aware of their own value systems, by demanding that the real problems tackled carry some risk of personal failure, so that the subjects can truly help each other to evaluate in what they may genuinely believe. (Revans, 1982)

Conclusion

The collaborative initiatives described in this article all have two major and parallel objectives in common: one is to explore means by which to provide all children with access to the curriculum; the other is to work collaboratively with colleagues both within school and within the support service to examine current practice and curriculum delivery with a view to improvement and development in the whole-school context.

Managing change 'entails amongst other things the willing participation of key personnel, a commitment to review and diagnosis, the identification of clear, meaningful and achievable goals, sufficient resources and a supportive social-psychological climate' (Bell and Pennington, 1988).

The crucial need to establish these 'minimal preconditions' has been reinforced consistently through earlier projects, where, certain of the above criteria were not adequately clarified. 'Action research and its characteristics are perceived as offering modes and **useful** steps into a research process which is not detached from other professional activities' (Silver, 1987). The development of action research modes of operation have therefore provided the members of this participative change cycle with a structure which facilitates reflection *and* action within a mutually supportive environment. Teachers involved in this work have displayed growing autonomy and leadership qualities in specific areas which have empowered them within their own institutions and within the developing network.

For some classteachers and support teachers, the opportunity to contribute to authority in-service courses has greatly enhanced their professional status and own sense of worth. One aspect of the hidden curriculum of such collegial work is the establishing of professional identity, improved self-confidence and consequently improved self-image within individuals which enables them to ' "become critical" — in the sense that they gather their intellectual and strategic capacities, focus them on a particular issue, engage them in critical examination of practice through the project' (Carr and Kemmis, 1986).

Some of the Outcomes So Far

(i) In all projects which are underway at various stages of the action plan there has always been, either implicitly or explicitly, a desire to effect change in the whole-school situation. For the practical purposes of managing such change, year groups **within** schools have been targeted, but with the managed involvement of others with cross responsibilities (e.g., for a curriculum area). Thus it has been possible to generate both interest and action in other areas of schools more speedily than anticipated. Power sharing has, in some instances, become a feature of school's functioning.

(ii) There is generally a raised awareness of children's needs and a pronounced enthusiasm to discover means by which to respond and fulfil the requirements.

(iii) Study of classroom management and the worthwhileness of the curriculum being offered, is clearly underway.

(iv) An increased sense of responsibility is discernible towards children, colleagues, the whole school *and* teachers' own professional development.

(v) More confident and active individuals within the schools and the support service are recognizing their power to influence thinking, activate others and to manage change, albeit slowly.

(vi) There is a growing recognition that change is a process of transition through which ground is gained in small, uneven steps and where consolidation and evaluation are vital ingredients for moving on.

Issues Still to be Addressed

A note of warning from Carr and Kemmis (1986):

> Once theories are regarded as already sufficiently justified and then applied uncritically, observation of their consequences is forgotten about.

The styles of support described in this account become incorporated into current practice and are continually influential in changing and developing the perceptions of all participants, whether involved directly or in a peripheral way. Consistent and structured evaluation of practice ensures identification of issues which require addressing, in terms of clarification, consolidation and development.

At present these issues include:

— The practicalities of resourcing, the maintenance of existing initiatives when the project mode is adopted in additional areas of the school.

— Activating new initiatives with adequate resourcing, particularly in terms of skilled and enthusiastic support staff.

— Sustaining and supporting both of the above.

— Providing adequate pastoral support for teachers involved in such work, particularly as the demands on them as individuals extend throughout the school.

— Reactivating the cycle to prepare and skill more staff jointly for engagement with collaborative styles of work.

— Extending the network whilst also sustaining the motivation of those currently involved.

---

1. The views expressed in this account are those of the author and do not necessarily represent the views of the Teaching Support Service of the LEA.

Appendix 1

Middle School / Teacher Support Service Collaborative Curriculum Development Project

1.0 *Project Objectives*
1.1 To provide support within the classroom for pupils with learning difficulties.
1.2 For staff to consider collaboratively the most effective means of meeting the curricula needs of pupils with learning difficulties.
1.3 In collaboration to develop approaches and resources appropriate to the needs of the pupil with learning difficulties.
1.4 To establish an approach designed to meet the needs of the pupils which can be adapted and adopted throughout the four years of the middle school.
1.5 To draw on the strengths of all staff, making effective use of their skills and experience.

2.0 *Why First Year?*
2.1 The existing timetable allows for the flexibility and cross-curricula approach required.
2.2 The First Year Team has considerable experience in the development of the integrated day which would considerably advantage the project envisaged.
2.3 Pupils moving from first schools would become involved immediately upon their entry into middle school and could carry the approach through with them as they progressed through the school.
2.4 It is now considered that staff have sufficient experience to be able to cope with the demands of meeting the needs of pupils with learning difficulties within the classroom. In the absence of the withdrawal group it is considered advantageous for additional support to be provided.
2.5 Large blocks of time are available for collaborative teaching to take place.
2.6 We are concentrating B. W.'s efforts into the First Year next year and his considerable primary experience will be invaluable in a project of this nature.

3.0 *Roles of Members of Project Team*
3.1 K. W. — Project Manager on behalf of the school.
Responsible for:

      (i)   Liaison between Project Team and headteacher.

      (ii)   Liaison between school staff and Teacher Support Service Staff.

      (iii) Motivation and support of Project Team.

      (iv) Facilitate possible developments into the Second Year.

3.2 M. M. — Project Manager on behalf of the Teacher Support Service.
Responsible for:

      (i)   Liaison between Teacher Support Service Staff and the Head of the Teacher Support Service.

      (ii)   Liaison between the Teacher Support Service and the school.

      (iii) General Administration of the Project.

      (iv) Producing minutes and agendas of meetings.

3.3 P. B. — First Year Leader — Classteacher.
Responsible for:

      (i)   Day-to-day organization and administration of the Project.

      (ii)   Initially Chairing meetings.

      (iii) Coordinating developments within the First Year Team.

3.4 P. L. — Special Needs Coordinator.
Responsible for:

      (i)   Maintaining an overview of the Project.

      (ii)   Relating Project objectives to proposed practice within the rest of the school.

      (iii) Being aware of the needs of pupils with learning difficulties within the First Year and their subsequent progress through the school.

3.5 M. T. — Humanities Coordinator — Classteacher.
Responsible for:

      (i)   Content of the humanities work to be covered throughout the project.

      (ii)   Resource management.

3.6 M. W. — Classteacher.

3.7 M. C. — CDT Coordinator. As this arrangement will require the input of another teacher into the First Year it is envisaged that this teacher will be a part of the Project.

3.8 B. W. — Teacher Support Service.
Responsible for:

    (i)   An input into the team of good primary practice in meeting the needs of pupils with learning difficulties.

4.0 *Project Organization — Timetable of Meetings*
4.1 10th May 1988 — Senior Staff Discussion.
4.2 17th May 1988 — Meeting — M. M., D. B., K. W.
4.3 20th May 1988 — Meeting at Teacher Support Service Centre.
4.4 7th June 1988 — Staff discussion at full Staff Meeting.
4.5 From 7th June 1988 until the end of term — weekly discussions for detailed planning.
4.6 September 1988 throughout the year — weekly or fortnightly discussions to discuss, plan, implement, monitor, analyze and evaluate project.

5.0 *Project Organization — Other Issues*
5.1 B. W. will concentrate his efforts within the First Year but will be timetabled into the Second Year for a small proportion of his time.
5.2 B. W. input into Second Year will be through setting individual work programmes for pupils in consultation with the classteacher. It is intended that this programme should be worked through within the classroom.
5.3 B. W. will retain the responsibility for evaluating the progress of all pupils currently receiving help from the Teacher Support Service.
5.4 P. L. will be timetabled to meet the needs of pupils with learning difficulties within the Third and Fourth Years.
5.5 The Project will need to be carefully evaluated. It is suggested this should happen at the end of each term. A formal written evaluation containing recommendations for the future will be produced on the completion of the Project.
5.6 Time will be made available for staff to visit other schools.
5.7 Considerations should be given to the use of Baker Days for the purposes of developing the project.

Chapter 9

Advisory Teacher Management: Towards an Entitlement Model

George Robinson

> If persons are to respond to instability and uncertainty, they must,
> on some basis, feel secure; a sense of personal security is essential to
> our ability to come to grips with change. (Schon, 1973)

Whilst a number of LEAs adopted an advisory teachers model several years before the Education Support Grant Programme (ESG) was launched, for the majority the ESG aided packages 'Mathematics in Schools' and 'Primary Science and Technology' provided the first real opportunity to advertise for a number of advisory support staff linked to a specified programme that included adequate resource funding. Therefore in 1985, LEAs were able to appoint a number of enthusiastic practitioners, on reasonably long-term contracts usually with a guarantee of at least a placement at the level of their previous substantive post at the end of the period of secondment. Being then employed as a General Adviser (Mathematics) in an LEA, I can still remember recognizing that after one year our team of five advisory teachers had probably made a greater impact on the quality of mathematics teaching, than two of us working as General Advisers over the previous seven. The emphasis suddenly switched from the after-school deficit model of INSET, three or four nights a week, to one of working with and alongside teachers during the working day supported by a well-resourced mathematics centre. The opportunity to provide supply cover for teacher release was an added bonus. Our role had changed from that of deliverer to facilitator.

The agreed statement issued by the officers' panel of the Soulbury Committee on 'The Role and Function of Advisory Teachers' amplifies a role expectation that is teacher focused:

> Advisory teachers function appropriately at the level of classroom
> practice, assisting teachers in the development of teaching skills,
> classroom management and resources. The advisory teacher should

operate as an 'expert teacher' capable of transmitting to others his own practical skills as a teacher and thus should be accountable to the Principal Inspector/Adviser. We believe that the work of the advisory teacher should be child/teacher/school based. (Soulbury Committee, 1989)

The panel went on to say that advisory teachers should not be expected to function at the level of an inspector or adviser and then listed areas of activity seen as being inappropriate for the postholders. Unrelated general administration, advice on appointment of staff, assessment and reporting on teaching competence and performance, advising on buildings, advising and inspecting on the whole curriculum, organization and staffing of educational establishments... all fell into the 'not appropriate' category. The role definition, therefore, enjoyed a certain neutrality through the exclusion of most of the more threatening inspectorial aspects of advisory work.

But, by defining the role for advisory teachers, the Soulbury Committee indirectly implied a significant role change for advisers, a shift that for many moved them away from the forefront of INSET and from the aspect of their work they enjoyed most. This change may have appeared to be sudden but in reality the pressures for readjusting priorities has been gradual over some ten to fifteen years. Bolam *et al.* noted in 1978 that a number of developments were 'pushing' the advisory service in the same direction, 'towards an evaluative, administrative, organizational and training-the-trainers role and away from advising individual teachers and direct participation in in-service training' and 'over the next few years they [advisers], too, may find themselves having to re-define their role as they carry out new tasks and as new groups in the profession carry out their old tasks' (Bolam, Smith and Canter, 1978). Without doubt the expansion of the ESG and LEATGS programmes has speeded up the process. Thus many advisers have, suddenly, during the past few years, found themselves with a line management responsibility for an 'expert' group of practitioners, fresh from the classroom, with high teacher and school credibility. At the same time the new appointees, in the majority of cases, needed to gain skills in new areas such as consultancy, working with adults and change strategies. These INSET imperatives of advisory teachers placed new demands on their line managers.

The change of emphasis for advisers from the 'missionary' deliverer to that of manager and training facilitator was for many far from easy and as more advisory teaching staff have been appointed it is not surprising that a whole range of management styles, management expectations and approaches to staff development have emerged. Whilst personally believing implicitly in growth through opportunity, the reality of our working world all too often stifles such development through daily pressures. 'A good planner plans time to plan' is a time management axiom that has an attractive ring of truth but how often do we actually achieve it ourselves, let alone deliberately create the time space for others?

In the case study that follows, issues faced by an LEA in initially expanding its INSET provision and at the same time investing heavily in an advisory teacher model, are highlighted. Three years later, management objectives for these advisory teachers are still being set and whilst some earlier problems remain, it is true to say that much has been learnt.

Sunderland, the largest of the five districts in the former Tyne and Wear Metropolitan Authority has a population of around 300,000 with a school population of 52,000. The area includes Washington which until recently was of new town status and has attracted a number of high tech-based enterprises as well as the Nissan car production plant. The LEATGS programme in 1987 facilitated the opening of the Broadway Centre for Educational Development occupying an ex-secondary school building, which was ideally situated in the centre of the Borough, providing easy access and potential parking for over 150 cars.

The plan involved moving all existing curriculum development units on to this single site and to attempt to establish a centre not too distant from the James Report's idea of a professional centre (DES, 1972). The concept was an exciting challenge for we were starting from scratch and at the same time, the introduction of the new INSET funding allowed the appointment of advisory teachers. Earlier assessment of schools' needs showed clearly a preference for the support teacher model. Broadway would, it was thought, also allow for a whole team approach and help to coordinate the work of the previously discrete bases. Units and services to be moved included the Inspectorate and Advisory Division, the TVEI Pilot and Extension Team, the Schools Curriculum Industry Partnership, the Science and Technology Regional Organization (SATRO), the Primary Science and Technology Centre, the Music Centre and its peripatetic staff, the Special Educational Needs Support Teacher Service and the Micro-Electronics Centre together with any support teachers already appointed under the ESG programmes. In addition, the building was to provide teacher centre facilities including an extensive resource library. Initial calculations seemed to indicate seventy plus staff with a secretarial pool of some nine or ten posts. In practice, we were attempting to move INSET from a fairly low position to one of high profile almost overnight. Current centre staffing now stands at over one hundred. New developments include a professional development unit, working to help schools in providing more effective INSET, and involving three to four seconded senior school managers, as well as a curriculum materials production unit and a timetabling base.

The first year now seems like a past nightmare. It was not wise, I was informed having been appointed in June, to leave the building empty over the summer holiday so the moves were scheduled two weeks before the end of the summer term. The school moved out on Friday and we moved in on Monday and Tuesday. Adaptations would take place with us in residence. Surveyors had weeks earlier decided that the flat roof needed renewing as well as remedial concrete work to the main external pillars of the three storey building. This was in addition to the internal alterations that were planned, ranging from the removal of science laboratories, electrical trunking of the whole building, installing a telephone system, providing adequate toilet facilities, to generally decorating and restoring a building that had been allowed to run down because of the pending closure. Hence, in that September over twenty of our newly appointed support staff (advisory teachers) found themselves temporarily in the hall with a single telephone from which one could rarely obtain an outgoing line. External noise and internal disturbances created almost unbearable working conditions. That first term saw the support team occupying three different bases before moving to their final new quarters. Fortunately TVEI was scheduled to move into Broadway later and Micro-electronics was postponed for a further two terms.

By the first Christmas, building difficulties were increasing rather than conditions improving as more work came on line. Complaints seemed to focus on noise, dust and smell. The support team was now housed in its second temporary home with a third move pending. The Advisory Service was experiencing similar problems. British Telecom had yet to deliver the new telephone system. One did not have to be particularly sensitive to know that all was not going well or that the climate was not conducive to establishing the ideal working relationships. The visibility of the support staff was also causing a problem. Some advisers started to check who were at their desks and asking questions as to why they were not out working in schools. Very different line management models were appearing. The contrast with the TVEI team, who had been working together for a considerable time, in some ways further aggravated the situation. Beliefs in self-responsibility within a working framework, of opportunity and space for growth and of a firm commitment to collaborative working at times seemed to be in a different world. Something had to be done.

The first move was to bring together a group of advisers and support staff to look at INSET for the support staff. At our first meeting we decided to hold a residential conference for the team in early May. The conference aim, through drawing on the collective expertise and experience of the course membership, was to examine and define, where possible, the framework for an effective support teacher provision. An expected outcome was to be the drafting of a document offering general guidelines to good working practice. A final follow-up meeting to share and collate findings was also planned in the middle of June.

It was agreed to form task groups to focus on specific aspects of support teacher work, i.e., (i) Induction (ii) Patterns of Working (iii) Personal Growth and Career Development (iv) The Supporting Environment (v) Measuring Effectiveness.

The Conference Programme was placed on offer and attracted excellent response with some thirty support teachers and a number of advisers applying.

The second move was to commission an LEA Support Teacher evaluation study to enhance the debate with the aim of illuminating the different perceptions, interests and judgments of the participants and to present a picture of the work of the support teachers within the current LEA context. Colin Biott of Newcastle Polytechnic and visiting fellow David Smith of the University of Sydney agreed to conduct the research study in a very tight time slot commencing at the residential conference in the first week of May and presenting the draft report at the follow-up day in middle June, thus allowing some six weeks for the study. An early decision was made to concentrate on the views of support teachers and LEA advisers.

Whilst these two initiatives were taking place after a period of surviving in the 'building upheaval', the end of the first phase of alterations was in sight. Newly decorated and carpeted rooms for the support teachers would soon be available.

The evaluators initially formulated the approach and the contract through negotiation with the support staff at the conference. The process was to include an analysis of the outcome of a prioritizing task, looking at positive and negative aspects of the job role, which was an integral part of the conference programme, use of an open-response questionnaire and then open-ended interviews without pre-structured questions but focusing to some extent upon issues raised in the first stages. A draft report would then be presented for validation before being finalized.

The recurring issues that emerged were:

— A supportive environment for support teachers both within the Broadway Centre and schools;
— The kinds of contact with schools that support teachers found satisfying or not satisfying;
— The future career of support teachers;

— Differences between support teachers and other teachers;
— Advice/information given to new appointees to support teacher posts in Sunderland LEA.

Probes were then chosen through analyzing the information for use in the subsequent interviews and these were:

— A supportive environment for support teachers
— The selection of support teachers
— How support teachers make contact with schools
— Profile of work of a support teacher
— Effectiveness criteria for support teachers' work
— Preparation of schools for support teachers
— Career of support teachers
— Management of support teachers
— Relationships between support teachers and the Advisory Service
— Future of the Advisers and Support Teacher Service in Sunderland Borough.

Whilst the final report (Biott and Smith, 1988) proved to be a very detailed and useful document, the following summary provided subsequently by the evaluators crystallized still further many of the issues.

Evaluation Report Summary

Problems arising from 'implicit judgments of effectiveness' and 'concern for personal credibility'

● Many support teachers are not being helped to replace the notion of 'credibility as a classteacher' with a concept of credibility as a 'support teacher' and this is causing concern for some of them when they are being marginalized by some school teachers. They were sometimes perplexed by the apparent inconsistency in expectations and they frequently guessed at the implicit criteria by which they were being judged.

Problems arising from dilemmas about 'support teaching' as a career step

● It was felt that the calibre of future candidates may be affected by the positions achieved by the current set of support teachers after their secondments were over. There was some speculation that some people were being dissuaded from applying for support teacher posts because it was felt to be an uncertain career step.

- The effect of the next career steps of existing support teachers on the future of the service was being seen as complex by both support teachers and advisers.
- Some of those interviewed were concerned that the job should not be seen as 'a standard' route to posts such as the LEA Advisory Service. It was suggested that the credibility of support teachers with classteachers would suffer if it was seen as a direct means of escape from the classroom.
- At the same time it was being recognized that support teachers were developing skills which could be used in future advisory roles. One compromise suggested was that some of those who return to the classroom could subsequently be successful applicants for advisory posts.
- Perhaps a variety of exit routes from the posts would serve to satisfy the career aspirations of support teachers and the importance of credibility in schools.
- The length of secondment and type of post were also thought to be affecting people's future career prospects. For example it was thought that a secondment of longer than three years may make it difficult for people to return to school.
- It was thought that single-subject primary school support may leave the support teachers feeling concerned about their ability to keep up to date in current developments in other areas of the curriculum.
- The complex set of issues heightens the importance of the relationship between advisers and support teachers as the latter rely to a considerable extent on the counselling, sponsorship and general stewardship of the former.

Problems in establishing worthwhile relationships with teachers

- Classroom work was being seen as important by all support teachers, but there was a general feeling that unrealistic expectations were being held about the time which it was possible for them to spend in classrooms engaged in work of significance.
- Many teachers do not wish to have support teachers in their classrooms, and of those who do many are likely to agree only to 'safe' work which is unthreatening and not challenging to themselves: demonstration lessons; working with a small number or group of children; accompanying a visit; providing resources or even 'cover'.

- For those support teachers working in cross-curricular areas, and for those concerned with new themes, additional time may be necessary in order to have their work accepted as part of an authentic agenda in the school.
- The LEA might recognize the difficulty support teachers have in establishing worthwhile, rather than superficial relationships, with teachers, and that appropriate groundwork may be essential before classroom work will lead to lasting change.

Problems arising from being concerned about immediate impact

- It was appreciated that 'flying visits' to conduct impressive lessons or staff workshops may be seductive. This could, especially, be a problem for ex-secondary school teachers working in primary schools where the children are reassuringly lively, responsive and interested. Progression in learning and in activities is harder to achieve and understand. It requires longer-term, reflective partnerships.
- Support teachers are vulnerable to becoming over-concerned with immediate impact as a result of being involved in many concurrent short-term school contacts, and not being able to study longer-term progression in children's/students' learning.
- The permanence of the advisers' positions is reflected in their long term views of the service. The seconded support teachers, on the other hand, tend to confine their views of the service to its immediate characteristics as they are currently being felt.

Problems about 'managing' support teachers

- The inspectors' and advisers' views of how the support teachers should be 'managed' perhaps reflect their views of the whole service of which they are a part. On the one hand there was a view that support teachers should be closely managed according to an agreed structure with clear parameters, on the other hand it was suggested that there should be a number of models to suit different purposes and to reflect different values. This was referred to, by one person, as a tension between the 'control' and 'enabling' aspects, which the advisers strive to reconcile in their own work. The former implies hierarchy, standard procedures, routines and uniformity. The latter emphasizes professional autonomy, equality, flexibility and diversity.

Problems arising from unequal advocacy for support teachers

- Some advisers talked enthusiastically about the successes of their own support teachers and that of the work of some others. This suggested that the advocacy skills of the adviser might be important:
  - (i) in helping the individual support teacher to build a sound reputation in the LEA and in schools during his or her secondment;
  - (ii) in providing important positive feedback to individual support teachers that is essential in the building of the confidence and self-esteem necessary for them to fulfill their roles;
  - (iii) in promoting a positive image of the support service in general, which also involves the nature of their responses to any ad hoc negative judgments which might be made in schools, either about a particular support teacher with whom they work directly or about other members of the support service; and,
  - (iv) in shaping the career prospects of individual support teachers in the Borough.
- The suggested importance of the place of advocacy of the support service by advisers raised questions of inequity amongst support teachers. (Biott and Smith, 1988)

Each of the Conference Task Groups, in the meantime, delivered positive and helpful working statements for the further development of the support teacher role.

The group looking at *Induction* saw it as an 'on-going' process blending gradually into the medium term INSET programme for support staff but initially recommended that an Induction Week should be held in the latter part of the summer term for the staff appointed to start in September. The aim was to give these staff an opportunity to familiarize themselves with the structures and procedures that relate to the service and to provide an opportunity to discuss and review current developments and policies. The group prepared a full programme which subsequently took place. The following year, the model was adjusted to a day in the summer term with the full week being the first week of the Autumn Term. This year, the planning group has arranged a fortnight's programme involving at times the full advisory and inspectorate service in looking at cross curricular issues such as assessment and teaching and learning styles.

Medium term developments were initially seen as

(a) Visits: Specific Institutions (e.g. tertiary colleges, special schools and the Enterprise Centre).
(b) Use of Resources with specific workshop sessions as required.
(c) Measuring Effectiveness: Review and Evaluation Skills.
(d) Peer and Mentor visits: Working with established support teachers.
(e) Support Teacher Skills: Consultancy Skills/Working with people/Management training,

and long-term developments included a work review, career guidance and specific career developmental activity. It is of interest to note that several of the medium developments are now incorporated into the initial training programme, particularly 'Use of resources' and 'Consultancy skills'.

The group considering *Patterns of Working* chose to offer two papers. The first provided information for institutions on the support teacher role whilst the second focused on the processes which supported the job role.

In the former, the point was made that the role of the support teacher is not easy to describe as work may take place in a variety of locations as a response to the needs identified by either individuals or institutions. Support, they thought, should be offered through a climate of partnership and collaboration which has the development of classroom processes as its primary aim. The group saw that from this, a number of principles of procedure may be established which describe a common pattern of working, although they pointed out that the listing should not be seen as exclusive nor hierarchical.

- To present positive and proactive stance to initiatives.
- To provide support for, face, challenge and initiate change.
- To highlight needs and opportunities.
- To enhance both the teaching and learning which take place in the classroom.
- To promote the development of a shared language and perceptions through involvement in a common experience.
- To plan, implement, review, assess and modify programmes with all concerned.
- To establish networks of communication and enhance cooperation and collaboration.
- To encourage dissemination and dialogue.

The eventual aim was to produce some case studies to aid the understanding of the role through which the different functions of a support teacher would, it was hoped, more clearly emerge.

In their second paper, the group offered the following five points to help ensure a service which was both dynamic and developmental in nature.

1 Support teachers were identified as those teachers appointed or seconded to work with teachers and institutions for the purpose of curriculum development and/or institutional change.
2 Regular meetings between support teachers and direct line management should form an integral feature of working practice.
3 The work of support teachers needs to be negotiated with individuals and institutions within a framework characterized by:
   (i)   the formulation of clear and shared objectives
   (ii) clarification and agreement of the support teacher's function
   (iii) collaboration and cooperation of all concerned
   (iv) review and evaluation as appropriate
   (v)   consideration of follow-up, as necessary
   (vi) continuity and progression.
4 The work of support teachers should be coordinated centrally and reviewed in both a personal and professional sense through contact with other support teachers, individual advisers, outside agencies.
5 The management of support teachers' time should allow for a degree of flexibility to include planning — implementation — review and evaluation of practice within particular contexts.

Some suggestions were then made which it was felt may prove appropriate to help facilitate the above. These were to:

— Identify a link person in each school/institution to coordinate support and establish collaborative working.
— Identify a pastoral coordinator for support teachers to assist with individual personal and professional development.
— Establish a bank of case studies to inform colleagues of practice within the support teacher service.
— Establish a forum for support teachers to meet, discuss and share ideas in order to generate more cooperative and creative provision across the curriculum.

It is of interest to reassess these points at this time for several developments are taking place. Although each school does have a nominated INSET coordinator, all too often the person is not aware of support staff involvement in the school. This issue is being tackled in current plans for the next phase of training for INSET coordinators. Similarly the 'pastoral coordinator' role is under review. As Senior Inspector (INSET), I have found myself considerably involved in individual personal and professional counselling whilst the Head of Centre has acted as coordinator for the INSET provision and convener of general meetings for the team. With over forty support staff there is a need to reconsider this situation. The whole team has been meeting monthly since the first conference providing a forum for discussing and sharing perceptions. Some case-study material of support teacher practice is to be included in the INSET coordinator folders currently being prepared.

The support teachers looking at *Personal Growth and Career Development* attempted to identify the features of provision that would facilitate the personal growth and career development.

They drew attention to:

1 Initial and on-going INSET to meet individual needs, e.g. specific curriculum contexts — skills associated with the role, e.g. consultancy.
2 Regular contact between support teachers to help develop their role.
3 Regular opportunities to share experiences and develop collaborative working relationships, with other members of the profession. Support teacher involvement in advance planning for the LEA.
4 Regular contact with advisers for appraisal, including — review of progress and setting new goals. (Covering personal, professional and support teacher development.)
5 Career counselling — prior to appointment
         — on entering and leaving the role
         — throughout the appointment
         — after the period of appointment
Should this be the role of a particular person?
e.g., Senior Inspector — INSET.
6 Opportunity to contribute to related developments at authority level beyond the period of appointment.
7 Support teacher role should be seen and used by the LEA as a means of personal and professional development.
8 An authority statement which describes the relationship between the support teacher service and the education service as a whole.
9 Opportunities to keep in contact with national developments and the provision of a library of resources.
10 Support in gaining further qualifications (e.g., part-time MEd) and training courses for re-entry to schools at higher level (e.g., management training for deputy heads).

They summarized their thinking in this statement:

The personal and professional development of support teachers is dependent on their effective implementation of the role. This must include time set aside for:
— forming relationships with individuals in schools;
— joint goal setting with partners in schools;
— implementation of programmes;
— review and feedback on the success of programmes;
— need for continued further involvement where appropriate.
An essential feature is self-evaluation and the production of evidence/case studies that will help others.

The group considering *The Supporting Environment* perhaps had the most difficult task for certain aspects were clearly going to be covered by other groups. Their statements however again added to the total picture.

1 *The nature of working relationships*

The right pattern of working relationships seems to be the key to a supporting environment. Trust is important within the LEA partnership of schools, support teachers and advisers. Developing these relationships should not be left to chance.

We need a structure which is underpinned at a number of stages by a process of NEGOTIATION and REVIEW.

Essential stages where this process would be employed are:

(i) between support teacher and adviser concerning initial and subsequent programmes of work.

(ii) between support teacher and school/institution concerning entry and role within school.

(iii) between support teacher and classteacher on the specific project in hand.

(iv) between support teacher and support teacher/team.

This model would promote:

(i) a 'protective' bureaucracy; that is, an established method of working which is helpful and efficient rather than cumbersome and time consuming.

(ii) an understanding of other roles.

(iii) through negotiation and review a practical and productive work load.

    (iv) collaborative work patterns.

    (v) the process of negotiation and review provides a ready mechanism for appraisal.

    (vi) team work and shared experience — although these may need specific development — for example, through the use of residential conferences.

2 *The physical environment*

If working relationships are right then the level of material support can seem less important. However, there is no reason why 'the base' should not be furnished to a professional standard and there is a need for clerical and technical support as well as reprographic and micro-processing equipment etc. The base should also provide support staff with somewhere to meet visitors.

3 *Communications*

Improved communications would come from the implementation of a negotiation and review structure.

The last group considered *Measuring Effectiveness*. In recognizing that the presentation of evidence of effectiveness depends on its content, the suggested framework for planning evaluation was 'What? Who? How? When? Where?'.

The underlying principles were seen as:

- Every support teacher has the responsibility to evaluate regularly the effectiveness of his or her work.
- This evaluation should provide feedback from which participants can learn.
- At the beginning of every support teacher's involvement in a project, objectives must be negotiated with other participants.
- These objectives should be attainable and measurable. Evidence of this should be produced.
- Evidence of a particular project belongs to the participants who set the objectives and worked to them.
- Use of this evidence outside of the group must be negotiated with the group.

After the conference, the initial planning group met again to arrange the follow-up day and to give consideration to its own role in the consultative framework. It proposed the following:

Name of Group   The group be called 'The Support Staff Advisory and Consultative Group' abbreviated to SSG for reference purposes.

Support Staff   For the purposes of the SSG, support staff be defined as teachers appointed to develop the curriculum through working predominantly with and alongside other teachers/lecturers and through INSET activity.

Composition   The core membership to consist of ten members, four being members of Inspectorate and Advisory Service (Chief Inspector nominations but to include Senior Inspector [INSET]) and four members of the support staff nominated by the support team plus the Head of Broadway Centre and the TVEI Coordinator. Whilst some continuity of membership is recognized as being advantageous, it is suggested that the membership be reviewed at the start of each academic year.

Meetings   The group to meet at least each half term. The meetings to have open access to interested parties.

Terms of Reference The following is not seen as a definitive list as the SSG will consider any issues related to support staff brought to its attention. Establishment of facilitating framework in particular to:
— provide and where necessary revise the support staff guidelines
— formulate support staff general policy statements
— develop team policies and collective working strategies
— provide a communication network and a forum to discuss relevant issues
— provide general INSET, the induction of new colleagues, and to assist in the 'return' process at the end of secondment
— consider appraisal and support staff development

—take responsibility for evaluating and monitoring the provision.

The framework was accepted by the Advisory Colleagues and the SSG came formally into existence. The group, besides receiving the commissioned evaluation report, has been very active in planning induction programmes, residential conferences and other INSET. The constitution has recently been amended to include a member of the professional development unit — the unit's staff have been working with support teachers in establishing a peer appraisal/development programme. A helpful outcome of the SSG has been to propose what has become known as the 'Entitlement Model'. To some the model may now seem to be rather bland but for us, at that stage of development, it served an important purpose.

Currently the model states:

The Individual Entitlement/Obligation

   (i) An LEA support teacher role statement outlining the 'role expectations' in general rather than subject specific terms. Mention to be made of the possibilities of subsequent consultative work for LEA after return to school.

   (ii) A curriculum brief (i.e., outlining more specific objectives particular to this post).

   (iii) A clear indication of the line management structure to appropriate named Adviser/Inspector or Management Group.

   (iv) Conditions of service including length of secondment.

   (v) An induction programme with the opportunities to participate in a continuing programme.

   (vi) Annual career advice and counselling as appropriate.

   (vii) A right to negotiate a phased 'return to school' programme in the final term of secondment.

The Releasing School Entitlement/Obligation

   (i) Secondment period to be agreed by the headteacher and the governing body and to be confirmed in writing.

   (ii) Cover (long-term temporary contract) to be allocated.

   (iii) Agreement to participate in the 're-entry' programme and to endeavour to use any enhanced skills the teacher may have developed.

LEA Entitlement/Obligation

   (i) To utilize the secondee within the terms of the contract and the funding regulations.

   (ii) To provide a professional supporting environment.

   (iii) To provide career advice and counselling on an annual basis.

   (iv) To provide appropriate training (INSET) during secondment.

   (v) To help schools to be aware of the role of support staff.

In reality much debate took place about appointment conditions and highlighted the responsibilities of the partners involved. The initial proposal included an entitlement for the support teacher during the first year of one half day per week for a negotiated study, research or task activity with the possibility of funding for an appropriate higher education course. The school would then have the right to negotiate, where appropriate, a school task or specific research study during the secondee's half day per week study activity. The LEA, it was suggested, could enjoy the same entitlement although it was expected that the majority of projects would be those of interest to, and chosen by, the individual support teacher. As an intermediate step a new Masters Degree has been negotiated with the local polytechnic and is currently being run at the Broadway Centre on an early evening basis. The course has been designed with sufficient flexibility to accommodate task and specific research studies and at the same time provide the academic rigour.

In addition, at this stage discussion explored the possibilities of subsequent consultative work for the LEA after the secondee returns to school and whether this should be seen as an entitlement or obligation for LEA and school. The first proposal was for so many days during the following year with the school having an entitlement to supply cover when this occurred. Issues such as these are still under consideration.

Practically all of INSET is now grant aided, principally through the LEATGS and ESG programmes together with the Training Agency's TVEI initiative. Each of these operate within clearly defined funding regulations and accountability procedures. Through these mechanisms the Secretary of State has encouraged local authorities to redeploy expenditure into nationally set priorities as well as in the case of LEATGS to allow considerable discretion for locally agreed imperatives. The funding programmes have facilitated a great deal of activity and much has been, and still is being, learned about delivering effective INSET. The majority of LEAs have positively influenced schools to accept self-responsibility for their INSET through delegating some of this money on a teacher pro rata basis: money which incidentally is not encompassed by the 'Local Management of

Schools' regulations for it is grant-aided and earmarked. The setting of long-term INSET aims and objectives, together with the implementation and subsequent review of provision, was a new challenge for most schools. It is noticeable that many are moving away from the initially adopted incrementalistic approach of meeting imperatives to one based upon long-term rationalization (Booth, 1988) through the setting of three or four year INSET plans — a movement that has been helped by the introduction more recently of whole-school development plans. At the same time, LEAs have similarly been developing more clearly defined long-term policy statements.

The specific aims of LEATGS set out in the circular of August 1989 for 1990–91 included 'to promote more systematic and purposeful planning of in-service training'. The HMI report on the first year of the scheme 1987–88, 'The Implementation of the Local Education Authority Training Grant Scheme' noted that 'the introduction of the LEATGS has resulted in more systematic approaches to the planning, organisation and delivery of INSET by the large majority of LEAs visited' and that 'in general terms INSET is now more healthy than it has been at any time previously, despite the various weaknesses identified in the first year of the new scheme'. Similarly the Efficiency Scrutiny of ESGs and LEATGs (January 1990) commented that the team was impressed by the energy and creativity which had been focused on INSET.

Ironically, one of the major problems being faced by LEAs is the apparent unpredictability of the funding structure and funding parameters together with the notification timetable that together forces one into short-term planning cycles. National Priorities, grant levels, accounting and bidding procedures have changed with very little warning. For example, for the financial year 1990–91, LEAs learnt in May 1989 that National Priorities had been dramatically reshaped, and in August 1989 that they were to lose nearly a third of their local priority area money: a loss of £261,000 for Sunderland. The final notification of amounts allocated were announced at the end of that Autumn Term, December 1989, allowing only the Spring Term for devising strategies to meet the new imperatives. Newly introduced priorities included: 20 day courses for Primary Science and Primary Mathematics; training for licensed and articled teachers; training in the management of pupils' behaviour and teacher appraisal. With this increase in national priority area money the grant level dropped from 70 per cent to 65 per cent thus effectively providing more national priority area money from the local priority areas budget, the latter of which is grant-aided at the lower rate of 50 per cent, for practically no extra government cost. Such cuts in local priority area funding affects the in-service infrastructure of which advisory teachers have become an important element — ESGs have the advantage of a defined life span although the grant support rate levels do change with significant drops in their later years (from 70 per cent to 50 per cent is not unusual). Newer ESGs have tended to be funded at 60 per cent rather than the previous 70 per cent level. The aim of providing 'systematic and purposeful planning' becomes increasingly more difficult to achieve against this changing backcloth.

It is not surprising that LEAs have appointed advisory teachers on short-term contracts simply on the unpredictability of the funding, although a recognized valuable asset of the appointee is that bank of recent experience capital which of course diminishes with time. Very short secondments require rapid skilling in job-related skills and even then leads to working to short-term objectives and hence incrementalism. Permanent appointments allows for the setting of long-term objectives at the cost of a diminishing relevant and recent classroom experience. Probably the ideal were those initiated as a result of the first ESG projects 'Mathematics in Schools' and 'Primary Science and Technology' where the life span was sufficient to allow appointments for two or three years with extensions subsequently being granted.

Local Management of Schools under the Education Reform Act 1988 legislation presents further difficulties. The new appointment procedure with the responsibility firmly placed with the school governing body makes redeployment extremely difficult and therefore any secondment will need to be from a specific school post rather than holding promises of a substantive post placement at the end of the contract. Will schools be prepared to release their 'expert' teacher, with a possible negative impact upon their own school, in order that the person can work with the staff of other schools which might be in direct competition for pupils? It is possible that release could help a school to achieve a budget balance or generate a needed surplus. If overstaffed, or if it is envisaged that the replacement might be at a lower salary level, there are definite cash benefits in agreeing to release a member of staff. But a problem arises with the replacement after two years — for employment protection legislation then comes into play: an unfair dismissal or redundancy case could be brought. The guarantee of a post back at school for the secondee can only be made in line with the security of other posts. Should a school be overstaffed, whose job is then safe? The staff member away from the school site may be in a very vulnerable position.

The Efficiency Scrutiny of ESG and LEATGS in noting some of these difficulties suggests that there might be a need for some form of incentive or inducement to schools to make it more attractive for them to agree to the secondment of members of their staff to advisory teacher posts.

Many advisory teachers would like to have extensions of current contracts and in most cases this would be to the advantage of the service. Unfortunately, the LMS and the employment protection legislation makes this an extremely difficult option. The offer of an advisory teacher to resign the school post and to take a chance at the end of the secondment does not help, for the LEA remains the employer and therefore unfair dismissal proceedings would still be possible. Some LEAs are overcoming the problems by advertising nationally and appointing to five 'school terms' fixed-contract posts with the intention of releasing the person before employment protection comes into play. Whilst one could argue this is not fair to the appointee, offering no long-term career development, perhaps we are moving into a period where advisory teachers will switch from LEA to LEA whenever the whistle is blown! Is five terms that much better than a one year secondment option, with the need to find a post at the end of the contract? The continuity of short-term secondments can be assisted through overlapping the replacement appointment so that the present incumbent helps to induct the new person in the dual appointment period. This model is being used in Sunderland with the Professional Development Unit where carefully negotiated two year secondments with a one term overlap takes place. With senior management appointments less difficulties seem to occur.

From the LEA viewpoint the least troublesome option is to contract an external consultant on a negotiated cost basis for a fixed term. But where are the consultants for the National Curriculum or for assessment? A recent survey by the Dorset County Assessment Unit found that the average number of advisory teachers per LEA was 40 — some 4,500 nationally — which indicates the size of the problem (Blanchard *et al.*, 1990).

Other options will need to be explored. A number of variants are possible. The release of a teacher for say a term to work within a cluster of schools with the agreement that each school involved will release one teacher consecutively for a term, could prove attractive to schools. The released teacher could be seen both as trainer and trainee working with colleagues in the group of schools.

Some LEAs have explored the alternative of appointing 'consultants' from their teaching force allowing ten days or so release in a year and paying that teacher an honorarium. This again comes up against the difficulty of acquiring the needed skills on the hoof and tends to miss the peer development that results from collaborative team work. Certainly there is mileage in appointing returned advisory teachers as part-time consultants — a step that would be welcomed by many current post holders.

The DES Project 'Raising Achievement in Mathematics' (RAMP) (1986–89) used a release pattern of one day per week over a three year period for their teacher–researchers (Ahmed and Williams, 1990). RAMP operated through a network of five regional centres to each of which was appointed a regional coordinator. The seventy teacher–researchers also participated in regional and national weekend conferences. The model provided a stimulus for growth and development, support and built-in after-care, meeting many of the requirements of a successful change agent. Initially, change is so easy to activate but then it is frequently left without a support mechanism and hence quickly dies. The support and challenge ethos generated by the regional group over the three years has led to some extremely successful curriculum development with a fundamental emphasis on autonomous self-development through a non-task orientated approach (Robinson, 1990).

Ideally the change agent needs to be indigenous to the client system and then to generate the change through an endogenous process — that is growth from within (Jones, 1969). There is a danger that the support teacher model can all too easily be seen as non-indigene and operate as an exogenous change agent through a tendency of providing centrally driven INSET rather than working with and alongside teachers in schools. Perhaps the answer may be in a part-time release model with the base school entitled to a considerable proportion of the teacher's time.

In Sunderland, our last residential conference for support staff tackled professional development from the personal viewpoint and then looked at new ways of achieving effective INSET. Much of the time for the latter was devoted to whole team/whole curriculum ways of working. Networking strategies both within the team, with advisers and inspectors, and with teachers in schools were seen as important.

I left the conference feeling tremendously impressed by the dedication and professionalism apparent and the high quality of the subgroup contributions. Across the country we have created a group of 'expert' change agents that will be lost if the government and LEAs do not quickly sort out the legislative tangle that currently exists. A solution is needed that will offer a real career path with personal security and progression.

Donald Schon (1973) in *Beyond the Stable State* wrote:

> At the root of most innovations significant enough to precipitate a change of state, there are individuals who display irrational commitment, extra-ordinary energy, a combativeness which enables them to battle established interests over long periods of time, and a remarkable skill at guerrilla warfare.

Advisory teachers have clearly demonstrated their value. It is now up to the managers to recognize that advisory teachers do have a deserved entitlement.

The School Context

Chapter 10

Advisory Teachers and School Development

Colin Biott

The final chapter draws together the strands of this volume and explores the role of advisory teachers in school development. In the lead book for this series, Holly and Southworth (1989) suggest that a school 'revolves around, and is energized by, its development culture'. This is defined as a school's organic 'capacity to move forward effectively and according to a particular style, a "house style" '. It is, they say, 'a question of generating the common understanding amongst staff that this is the way we go forward in this school' (p. 24). Evaluation, collaboration and learning are the essential features of this development culture. The learning, they describe, is about doing. It includes children's learning, teachers' learning which is both individual and collaborative, and also organizational learning.

The emphasis, then, is upon the school's efforts to enhance its own learning capacity and to derive benefits from its own thoughts and actions. In this sense, school improvement grows from the inside, and this raises questions about the ways in which external advisory or support teachers have contributed, or may contribute, to its processes. Even though much has been achieved already, it is still important to exercise caution and to avoid being over-simplistic in claiming lasting success.

In Chapter 3 questions were raised about the extent to which semi-detached teaching may be a rewarding career phase, and the discussion mainly considered the LEA context, and the way in which the advisory teachers might learn from working with each other. In this chapter the emphasis has moved to the many different school contexts in which the advisory teachers attempt their work, and the focus has shifted to the learning benefits of the host teachers and schools. Like McLaughlan and Yee (1988), Joyce and McKibbin (1982) have considered how different school environments are likely to either foster or restrict teachers' professional growth. They have referred to three types of schools: 'the self-actualizing school', the 'comfort school' and the 'survival school'. This is a useful categorization for beginning to consider advisory teachers' roles in school development.

The Self-Actualizing School has the following characteristics:

- A free and strong interchange of ideas — with some ideas being trawled from outside, considered with seriousness and taken on their merits.
- Considerable energy being expended on self-development.
- Warm, informal interchange which fosters more growth — producing activities by individuals, small groups and the staff as a whole.
- Change efforts are supported by the strong, formal system of the school.
- The school has a strong, formal in-service programme which caters for both institutional and individual needs.
- Advisory/support staff are deployed effectively, so that they can interact productively with staff members.

The Comfort School has a semi-positive orientation to change, but efforts are fragmented rather than collective. It is described as 'supportive but not synergistic'.

The Survival School has a negative environment which works against change, and blocks the release of energy. It is characterized by:

- Individual members of staff feeling that they have to be covert about their personal efforts, their isolation thus cocooning them against the ridicule of colleagues.
- Phobic reactions to the possibility of change.

Making use of this categorization of schools, it follows that the criteria for judging successful advisory or support work will differ according to the characteristics of the host schools. It suggests that the pre-conditions should be taken into account before support strategies are planned. In a 'survival school', for example, any limited success is likely to be gained with individuals and to be kept private, as in the case quoted in Chapter 2:

> she was a lovely person to work with in the classroom, but she ignored me in the staffroom. I stopped trying to talk to her in there. (ESG support teacher)

That classteacher's personal engagement with new developments in her own classroom and her partnership with the advisory teacher were being kept separate from her role as an apparently self-sufficient school colleague. During the early stages of the evaluation of that project, some teachers were also unwilling to have their positive comments released to other teachers in the school. There was a general and enduring resistance to the externally imposed initiative, and this inhibited the collective celebration of any subsequent benefits. In such schools, the advisory teachers' contributions seemed mimimal at first, although they did offer opportunities for some teachers to have experience of learning partnerships in their own classrooms. The advisory teachers also became interested listeners when some teachers wanted to talk about their professional enthusiasms in a way that would be inappropriate with their own colleagues. Perhaps the value of this should not be underestimated.

Frustrations are also likely to arise when too much is attempted in what has been called a 'comfort school'. For instance, advisory teachers for cross-curricular themes may find some receptive and responsive departments or sections in a 'comfort school', but their efforts may have limited scope because of the lack of whole-school coordination. There is evidence of this, for instance, in the following personal evaluation record of a support teacher for 'language across the curriculum' in secondary schools:

IN THE BEGINNING

My major problem in the beginning was one of access. To some extent it still is a problem and this is something which needs to be addressed if the strategy is to be employed for a further two years.

First of all I had to work across the whole curriculum which meant that I had to work with strangers. Obviously I know many English teachers in the LEA but very few from other areas of the curriculum. Furthermore, when you are coming into another teacher's subject you are looked upon as lacking in expertise in that particular subject. The other element, and the one which caused the most problems, was the schools themselves and their perceptions of what I was doing.

In spite of having agreed that the development of language across the curriculum policies was to be part of the extension, schools generally have given it a very low priority. Not one school decided to take this on at a high enough level. As a result I often found myself nibbling around the edges and never getting to the meat in some of the early projects with which I became involved.

After it became clear that schools were not going to assist access in any meaningful way I set about trying to identify teachers who had an interest in language across the curriculum. This was done by enlisting the help of advisers, advisory teachers, deputy heads and whoever I met on the various courses I attended. Once identified, the teachers were invited to a language across the curriculum course. If they came I then endeavoured to make an appointment with them to see if I could help them identify their own needs. When we next met we discussed how I could help the teacher concerned. I then went away, produced some ideas, returned, negotiated and fixed a date to run a pilot programme. The next step after the pilot was to fix a date for evaluation, do the evaluation and then see how we could move on from there so that the teacher would embed language development in ordinary lessons. This sometimes meant producing an outline for a series of lessons.

Once entry had been gained it often meant that other teachers would become interested and would ask for help. This probably explains why I have been far more active in some schools than in others. Also, of course, you have to go where you are welcome.

CURRENT SITUATION

Generally, schools have approached the development of language across the curriculum in two ways. About half of secondary schools have appointed LAC coordinators and/or have established working groups which are focusing on various aspects of language. A common approach is to narrow the field down to one area and one year group; for example, looking at and then formulating a school policy for spelling in the first year. All of these developments have been supported either indirectly through centre-based INSET and as a resource for materials, or directly through school-based INSET by working alongside teachers in classrooms.

Other schools which have not yet appointed LAC coordinators have sent staff to LAC courses and this has often been the starting point for school-based INSET. I have worked directly in these schools and sometimes across several subjects. Across the LEA the subjects involved have been English, mathematics, science, history, geography, PSE, home economics (food studies, textiles, child development) and technology.

In view of the importance placed on language in the National Curriculum documents on Science, Mathematics and Technology, as well as, obviously, English, the project has been re-named Language Across the National Curriculum. Perhaps schools will now see the development of language policies as being important. Actually they now have no choice; it is a NCC requirement.

FUTURE DEVELOPMENTS

I would like to place more emphasis on the development of spoken language as an agent of learning over the next phase. Due to difficulties which I have already described above I have been unable to give this aspect of Language Across the National Curriculum the attention it deserves.

The major problem with the project is the one which has never gone away: unless schools make access easier and decide that the development and implementation of whole-school policies (now a NCC requirement) is something to be taken on at the highest level, and, therefore, given the full backing of management, then the development of the project will continue to be piecemeal.

The appointment of LAC coordinators and the establishment of working groups is to be welcomed. It is a pity, however, that apart from doing INSET with some of the working groups, I have not, with one notable exception, been made a member of these groups. As a resource I do feel that I have been undervalued and underused.

For the future I think that a good way of working would be as follows:

1 invite me to a meeting of the Language and Learning Committee;
2 discuss an appropriate way of using me in school to help implement a whole-school policy;
3 set short-term and long-term targets;
4 draw up a contract showing the duration of the project, the targets to be met, the input required from myself, and the school's contribution;
5 build evaluation into the project;
6 set dates for a review (more than one may be required if the project lasts for half a term or more); and
7 decide on the next move.

If schools do not as yet have Language and Learning Committees then I will be pleased to help them set them up.

This extract from a personal evaluation record illustrates how an advisory teacher can feel 'undervalued and underused', partly because of difficulties of access, partly because of lack of coordination within schools and partly because of the way in which the role remains marginal to the school's own working group or committee structures. Sometimes advisory teachers have committed a great deal of time and effort into working in a school only to find that their field of interest is of low priority for many of the staff at that time. This is, to some extent, the result of both internal and external fragmentation of effort.

In primary schools in particular, curriculum coordination is problematic and likely to become even more so as the National Curriculum unfolds and more subject areas demand increased staff development time. Even with the necessary expertise and personal qualities, how many school curriculum leaders can be concurrently carrying out their roles effectively? Without internal support, overall coordination and careful phasing, it is likely that their impact may be piecemeal and shallow. At the same time, how many advisory teachers will have the opportunity to work in schools which have made their areas of interest the main focus for development over an extended period of time?

Fullan (1988) has advised schools to avoid 'random learning' during a time when there is constant bombardment of change from the outside. He suggests that it is useful to have a 'critical screen' to sift out what is untimely and to allow for concentrated effort on what the school staff identifies as important. As an example of this, a primary headteacher indicated, during an evaluation study of an ESG Primary Science and Technology Project, that she would not want the advisory teachers to do any teaching in her school during the next phase of the project. The school was fairly confident about its teaching of science and so she said that:

> The first stage would take place in the term prior to the main support work being undertaken. The support teacher would attend meetings of the school staff and develop an over-view of science work in the school, especially the school's aspirations to improve or extend aspects of its work.

> The clarification of purpose and the establishing of patterns of support teacher involvement would take place over an extended time period. It would be the intention to include all teachers in the planning phases so that none would feel 'left out' or isolated.

> The teachers in the school would plan to work on a common theme, and the support teacher's involvement would be for a whole term, and ideally for one day each week.

The most worthwhile activity for the support teacher at the present time would be to observe and collect evidence of the science work in action in classrooms.

'The classrooms would be the workshops'.

The evidence, such as observation field notes, children's work or recordings of interaction, would be available for staff evaluation sessions. The support teacher would also participate and become aware of what further evidence was required to elucidate the next questions or issues arising from the agreed action.

This way of working, it was thought, would empower the teachers and be more likely to have a lasting effect upon the school's practice.

Joyce and McKibbin's (1982) concept of the 'self-actualizing school' is close to what Holly and Southworth (1989) have called the 'learning school'. Unlike the 'survival' or 'comfort' schools it seems to offer opportunities for external advisory or support teachers to convert their efforts into meaningful, collaborative learning activity which will have depth, direction and continuity for the whole school. However, before returning to this issue in more detail, it is useful to consider the idea of a school's readiness for external support. A key question is whether an external support project can establish the conditions for success which were absent at the outset, or whether a school's capacity to benefit remains dependent upon its prior state of readiness; the pre-conditions. The following evidence from a case study of three schools does suggest that it may be possible to accelerate a school's momentum towards becoming a 'learning school' as an integral part of the processes of a project. Just as the role of advisory teaching has been developing, over the past decade, through the trial and error of experience and practice, so have some schools been transforming their cultures through the challenges, discomforts and anxieties of being targeted for external support for which they were not ready and which they did not seek. The following critical history of a project illustrates this point.

The Critical History of a Project

This case study is based upon a two and a half year evaluation study of an ESG Urban Primary School Project in three schools. After having offered critical support to what, at different times, seemed to be its most vulnerable participants, I tried, as the evaluator, to prepare a historical account of the project which would represent all viewpoints and maintain the dignity of all groups. The project history was seen as a way of setting negative actions and reactions in time. It allowed me to write about weaknesses, failures and resentments in a constructive form. This involved a great deal of checking and cross-checking. A draft version was discussed and cleared by the project steering group and then given to the participating teachers for further comment. In this way, the last word was given to the teachers and their views were added to the final evaluation report. The main phases are summarized briefly here.

1985—1986

Being Targeted: Suspicion, Defence and Hostility

Because of the short time-scale for bidding for national funds, the LEA did not have enough time for thorough and extensive consultation and negotiation with the three targeted schools. The teachers' hostility towards the idea of the project was further increased both by the advertisement for the project team members, who, it was said, 'would improve their schools', and by the aims document which stated, amongst other things, that the team would raise their expectations. The difficulties of the new project team were compounded by the current· industrial action, and as a teacher said to them, 'You're like a red rag to a bull in there!'

Running with Buckets: Overcoming the Bad Start

During the first year of the project, the team and many of the teachers were working hard to overcome the bad start. The team's work was later described as 'running with buckets' — an extension of the metaphor — 'you can take a horse to water, but you can't make it drink'. In this case, the water (in the form of support) was being taken to the horses (the classteachers). Some seemed a little thirsty, some took a cautious drink and others refused to sip. The teachers' views of the project were surveyed, and this indicated that, after two terms, only two of the thirty-eight teachers said that they felt deeply involved in the project, twenty-two said that they were marginally involved and fourteen said that they were not yet involved at all. There was much doubt, at that time, about whether the project would yield any long-term benefits:

If it failed the present teachers would be expected to pick up the pieces. If it was successful, how could the staff be expected to maintain the activities which have required extra finance and staff?

September–October 1986

Consultation and Participation in Planning and Review

In response to the survey results, the steering group decided at this stage to attempt to re-orientate the project so that the schools would have a sense of 'ownership'. The focus for the increased participation and responsibility was the planning of INSET activities. It was agreed that:

- Each school would set its INSET priorities.
- Each school would have a staff member involved in the group which was planning and reviewing INSET.
- The timescale should be short to avoid loss of enthusiasm.
- The school representatives on the planning group should lead the consultative dicussions in their own schools.

January–February 1987

Collegiality and the Project Team as Learners

At this time headteachers were reporting that the project was 'affecting the amount and the intensity of staff discussion' in the schools. Attention was moving towards the aim of generating 'a collegial approach to change'. This was considered, by the steering group, to be a worthwhile and tolerable modification rather than a redefinition of the project aims. Questions were being raised about whether the increased involvement of some staff was serving to harden the resistance of others, and ways were being sought to facilitate any change of stance of those who had set themselves explicitly and assertively against the project.

By focusing on the collaborative involvement of the staffs of the schools the emphasis was being shifted into areas in which the project team could have little direct influence. It could not initiate or lead this kind of development. The project team members were now indicating that they were learning a great deal through collaborating and talking with teachers in the schools. In successful partnerships they said that they felt like colleagues, having genuinely lost the 'expert' label, which was nevertheless still being used by some classteachers who continued to maintain their distance from the project.

March 1987

A Form of Self-Evaluation for Headteachers?

After a whole-day planning meeting one of the headteachers said that the project had become a 'form of self-evaluation for headteachers'. It was becoming even clearer that it was not enough for a few individuals to benefit, but that the project should affect the culture of the whole school. At the same time it was agreed that the project teachers would not be expected to establish working relationships with all of the teachers in the schools, as it was thought that this would waste some of their time and energy in fragmented effort. Instead, they would concentrate on the pockets of teamwork and work at developing effective support roles within teams.

At this time, the strong and weak aspects of the project were being compared. The strong aspects were where the classteachers and support teachers were sharing the tasks of planning, teaching and reviewing. They were thinking aloud together about children's learning progress, and they were learning themselves through joint experience and dialogue. As a result, longer term professional development needs were being discussed. The weaker side of the project, however, was still characterized by an exclusive and pragmatic emphasis on the decontextualized provision of resources, on meeting immediate resource needs, and on giving 'cover' or being an 'extra pair of hands' with no subsequent reflection or review.

Curriculum Leaders as Project Leaders
Project Team as Support

The main intention at this stage was that the project should become embedded in the formal practices of the school, and the school curriculum leaders should take responsibility for initiating and sustaining development activities. The following set of guiding principles was established at that time:

1 Teachers should have the opportunity to work with another

teacher in their own classrooms. It was agreed that 'shared planning', teaching and reflecting is the central aim. Colleagues on the school staff could be partners (not just the project team). The talk between the partners should be mainly about the children's learning (rather than classroom organization).

2   The school staff should be involved in project planning.

3   Planning and evaluating time should be made available, and recognized as important, for discussions between teachers, between teachers and 'the team', between teachers and the headteachers, and within the team itself.

4   Processes of dissemination and liaison between the schools should help to give the project its coherence, during a period in which the separate schools might have different needs for support.

5   Thought should continuously be given to forming a base for continuity and development within the schools after the end of this project. People with leadership responsibilities should develop their approaches to working with colleagues through being given some additional time, support and opportunity for sharing reflections. Staff should become more convinced of the value of talking, thinking and learning together.

March 1988

What Has the LEA Learned?

The headteachers had seen convincing evidence of the impact of the project in their own schools, but they were now anticipating some difficulties in maintaining future momentum without external resources and support. Questions were being asked about how the LEA would continue to help after the end of the project, and whether it would review and clarify its own support framework in light of the experience of the project.

At the same time, the headteachers were beginning to consider the steps that they might take to maintain the links between the three schools. They talked about teacher interchange and collaboration and about sharing resources. They felt that they had established confidence and trust in each other through their involvement in the steering group. As one said:

I didn't feel like a stranger when I was in your school.

This case study has been included to illustrate how the lack of readiness of the schools and the absence of a period of preparation affected the course of the project's development. The project was susequently shaped by the emergent aims which emphasized ownership, collegiality and continuity. What was achieved should not be judged solely on the basis of the initial, imposed and decontextualized, national project aims. In particular, the project had:

— accelerated developments in children's, teachers' and the org-
    anization's learning which could not have been attempted
    concurrently without special support;
— enhanced understanding, within the schools, of how external
    support might be used;
— provided a learning forum for headteachers to discuss the dilemmas
    and problems of sustaining school developments, and for them to
    benefit from understanding the nature of the divergence and
    common ground between their schools;
— offered some of the teachers the opportunities to gain experience of
    learning in partnership with colleagues;
— given the advisory teachers the opportunities to reflect upon their
    work through discussions with headteachers, LEA advisers and an
    independent evaluator;
— helped the headteachers to realize the internal collaboration and
    support potential of their schools;
— suggested ways in which the LEA might organize its support
    frameworks in order to assist schools which are at the same starting
    point as those in the project.

A number of lessons have been learned, during the past decade, about how semi-detached teachers might best support school development. The above example has been included to show how the potential benefits cannot always be identified precisely at the planning stage. It also suggests that with perseverance it is possible to make progress from different starting points and to overcome early difficulties. This seems to require resilient, adaptable advisory teachers and host teachers, an adequate time-scale, mutual support arrangements for the headteachers, the steady stewardship of LEA advisers, and perhaps the additional help of an independent, formative evaluator. In addition to patient support it also seems important to protect the participants from inappropriate or premature assessments of what is being achieved. The schools should set their own realistic targets about which there is sufficient agreement for checks on progress to be meaningful and enabling. Such an undertaking is expensive, however, and it is more usual to suggest that the pre-conditions for success should already exist at the outset. Webb (1989), for instance, has said that:

> crucial to the success of the language advisory teachers' new approach, was an appropriate organizational climate where staff were used to confiding in one another and sharing ideas, and where the headteacher was already committed to developing a more participatory style of management. (pp. 49–50)

She has identified a number of factors from her study of the work of a team of language support teachers, which could help primary headteachers who intend to use external support through consultancy-based INSET:

1   The importance of not being over-ambitious, particularly in the first instance, and the need to identify a specific project goal that can be achieved realistically within the time-scale of one or two terms' work.

2   The need to negotiate the focus, duration, nature of staff involvement and the resources required by the project with the consultant and all the staff — possibly through an exploratory meeting.

3   The value of a contract, which is considered satisfactory by all involved, and drawn up well before the start of the project with the understanding that it may be renegotiated if, and when, necessary.

4   An awareness on the part of the headteacher that the project's review process, particularly if it involves classroom observation, may be threatening to classteachers. They are likely to require support and encouragement during this period of insecurity. Also, the project may reveal unanticipated problematic aspects of the school's management and communication systems.

5   An acknowledgement of how far the processes involved in the project's collaborative review and decision-making represent a departure from the norm. An awareness that the headteacher and the staff may need to develop new organisational and interpersonal skills as well as those associated with the project innovation.

6   The need to ensure that time is set aside — either during the school day or after school — for those involved in the project to discuss progress and difficulties with each other and the consultant.

7   The desirability, where new methods of teaching and learning are being introduced, that teachers should have the opportunity to work with the consultant and/or colleagues who have already incorporated the new ideas into their classroom practice.

8 The need to ensure that there are formal as well as informal ways of reporting the work of the project group to the rest of the staff, disseminating findings and encouraging staff who have not been involved to adopt the resultant ideas, policies or curricular materials. (Webb, 1989, p. 50)

By drawing attention to the importance of setting realistic goals and of clarifying the focus, nature and duration of staff involvement, she points, like McKenna in Chapter 8 of this volume, to the value of a contract. At the same time, she stresses the need to recognize that the contract may be re-negotiated when necessary. This seems to be important in the light of the case study described above. A project which begins to have impact on a school's learning capacity is likely to continue to develop in ways which were not fully anticipated at the outset, especially when the school does not already have the characteristics of a 'self-actualizing' or 'learning school'. Holly and Southworth's (1989) concept of the Developing School is important here. It is not a Develop*ed* School but a Develop*ing* School, which provides the best context for advisory teachers' work.

Looking to the Future

In the first chapter, advisory or support teaching was described as an uncertain role which had grown in an ad hoc way through a range of projects in the 1980s. During this period many of these semi-detached teachers had tried to give support to some teachers and schools who were not ready to make use of it, and who resented the idea of outsiders meddling in their work. On the other hand, in parallel, and sometimes related to the same projects, there had been an increase in the number of schools which had already been formulating 'development plans'. These schools were placing themselves in a stronger position to seek specific help and to benefit from the availability of external support.

The idea of development planning in schools was not new when the ILEA made it explicit in 1985 (ILEA, 1985). It was then given further impetus when the House of Commons Select Committee Report (1986) recommended that all primary schools should be 'required to operate according to development plans agreed with the governing body and the LEA'. More recently, the School Development Plans Project has produced a booklet (DES, 1989d) which gives advice to governors, headteachers and teachers. It encourages them to ask questions about where the school is now, what changes it needs to make, how the changes might be managed over time and how it will know whether the management of change has been successful.

At the beginning of the 1990s the preparation of school development plans is seen as important in view of the rapid pace of change. Schools need to guard against becoming overwhelmed by trying to do too much too quickly. The processes of formulating corporate plans should help in the setting of realistic short-term goals whilst encouraging a sense of long-term development. The coordination of financial planning, curriculum planning and staff development will be needed to enable a school to meet the statutory requirements of the Education Reform Act and the National Curriculum, as well as to establish its own priorities. As a result of this, requests or bids for advisory teachers' support should become more clearly focused in future.

The aggregation of schools' development plans by LEAs will put them in a better position to review, plan and manage their own support services. At the same time, steps are being taken to make national INSET initiatives more coherent by introducing a unified system to replace the previously separate LEATGS and ESG grant systems. This should lead to a rolling programme of activities with more defined periods of support. Further coordination is also desirable so that LEAs and schools may make best use of the various contributions to INSET strategies and materials from the DES, HMI, the National Curriculum Council (NCC) and Schools Examinations and Assessment Council (SEAC). The longer-term result of these trends should be for LEAs to have a clearer idea of how to define the role of their advisory teachers in relation to other groups in the overall service, and how best to prepare them for their tasks. These were both factors which the HMI said required urgent attention during the first year of LEATGS in 1987 (DES, 1989b, para. 3.16).

This volume, as a whole, has reviewed some of the difficulties and weaknesses of the work of semi-detached, advisory teachers, and indicated some of its successes and strengths. The intention has been to acknowledge the complexities of the role and to contribute towards an enhanced understanding of its nature over the past decade and particularly over the last five years. Much has changed during that time, and a great deal has been learned from experience. The practice of advisory teaching has been shaped to a great extent by environmental factors at national, LEA and school levels, and that is likely to continue. At the time of completing this volume, there was much speculation about the effects of the Local Management of Schools (LMS) upon the future of advisory teaching. On the one hand, there were doubts about whether schools would release their most able practitioners, and on the other hand, there was an indication that some schools may wish to second their most highly paid members to the LEA for a specified period in order to save money.

The need to save money may also lead to schools ignoring opportunities for outside help. However, with more schools formulating explicit School Development Plans and with the improved coordination of LEA professional support services, the context for advisory teaching is improving. Further steps still need to be taken to facilitate movement between key posts in different parts of the education service. If that were to be made possible, then for many teachers a period of semi-detachment in an advisory capacity would be an even more rewarding career phase. Advisory teachers learn fast and they often become even more valuable assets to the profession after their term of secondment is over. It is important that we continue to offer opportunities for lateral extension, in order to nourish the future development of mid-career teachers of such quality.

Notes on Contributors

Colin Biott is a principal lecturer in Educational Development and Enquiry at Newcastle Polytechnic. Previously, he taught in primary and secondary schools. He is the course leader of the modular MEd programme and he has been extensively involved in research and evaluation projects in LEAs. He is currently a member of the National Curriculum Council Professional Development Committee.

Mike Sullivan is the headteacher of Busill Jones Primary School in Walsall. He is one of the editors of *Education 3–13* and a frequent contributor to educational publications.

Graham Atkinson is a support teacher for special educational needs in a large comprehensive school. He was recently a support teacher for the humanities in primary and secondary schools.

Bridget Somekh is senior research associate at the Centre for Applied Research in Education at the University of East Anglia. Currently she is the director of the Initial Teacher Education and New Technology Project and coordinator of the Classroom Action Research Network. She was closely involved in the training of advisory teachers for the ESG Information Technology Project.

Patrick Easen is currently the coordinator of school-centred INSET at the University of Newcastle. He works extensively with primary school teachers in school-based and other forms of INSET. Prior to this, he was a tutor at the Open University and a primary school teacher.

Maggie McKenna is deputy head of the Doncaster Teaching Support Service. Prior to that she had wide teaching experience in primary and secondary schools and in further education.

George Robinson is currently the senior inspector for In-Service Education in the Borough of Sunderland. Previously, he taught in primary and secondary schools in Bedfordshire, Surrey and Devon, was the first warden of West Gloucestershire Teachers Centre and a general adviser in Cleveland LEA.

Bibliography

AHMED, A. and WILLIAMS, H. (1990) 'Raising achievement in mathematics project 1988–89', DES.

ALEXANDER, R. (1984) *Primary Teaching*, London, Holt Rinehart and Winston.

ALMOND, L. (1982) 'Containable Time', Appendix in *Institutional Self-Evaluation*, Block 2, Part 2 of Course E364 (Curriculum Evaluation and Assessment in Educational Institutions), Milton Keynes, Open University.

BELL, G. M. (1985) 'INSET-5 types of collaboration and consultancy', *School Organisation*, 5, 3, pp. 247–56.

BELL, G. M. and PENNINGTON, G. (1988) 'Action learning and school focused study', published K. M. Clyburn — Department Management Studies, Teesside Polytechnic.

BICKLEN, S. K. (1986) 'I have always worked: Elementary school teaching as a career', *Phi Delta Kappa*, 67, 7, pp. 504–12.

BIOTT, C. and SMITH, D. (1988) 'It's Early Days Yet: Towards Building Effective Support Teacher Roles', Sunderland LEA (obtainable from: The Broadway Centre, Springwell Road, Sunderland).

BLANCHARD, J., COWLING, L. and NEWHOFER, F. (1990) 'A Changing Role for Advisory Teachers?', Mimeographed paper: Dorset County Assessment Unit, May.

BOLAM, R., SMITH, G. and CANTER, H. (1978) 'LEA Advisers and the Mechanisms of Innovation', NFER.

DE BOO, M. (1988) 'Supporting science: Reflections of an advisory teacher', *Education 3-13*, October, pp. 12–17.

BOOTH, T. (1988) *Developing Policy Reseach*, Gover.

BRANDES, D. and GINNIS, P. (1986) *A Guide to Student-Centred Learning*, Oxford, Blackwell.

CAMPBELL, R. J. (1985) *Developing the Primary School Curriculum*, London, Holt Rinehart and Winston.

CARR, W. and KEMMIS, S. (1986) *Becoming Critical: Education Knowledge and Action Research*, Lewes, Falmer Press, pp. 40–1.

DAVIES, J. D. and DAVIES, P. (1988) 'Developing credibility as a support and advisory teacher', *Support Learning*, 3, 1, pp. 12–15.

DAVIES, R. *et al* (1988) 'Team management', *Marketing Intelligence and Planning*, Vol. 6, No. 1, pp. 32–9.

DENSCOMBE, M. (1983) 'Interviews, accounts and ethnographic research on teachers', in HAMMERSLEY, M. (Ed.) *The Ethnography of Schooling*, Driffield, Croom Helm.

DEPARTMENT OF EDUCATION AND SCIENCE EFFICIENCY UNIT (1990) *A Scrutiny of ESG and LEATGS*, DES.

DES *Report by H.M. Inspectors on the Implementation of LEATGS: The First Year of the Scheme 1987-88*, HMSO.

DES (1972) *Teacher Education and Training*, (The James Report), HMSO.

DES (1989a) *Improving Urban Primary Schools. A Report on an Education Support Grant*, Report by HMI, INS 56/12/284 78/79 NS 60/87, HMSO.

DES (1989b) *The Implementation of the Local Education Authority Training Grant Scheme (LEATGS): Report on the First Year of the Scheme*, Report by HMI, INS/56/12/301 136/89 NS 69/87, HMSO.

DES (1989c) *A Survey of Support Services for Special Educational Needs*, Report by HMI, INS/56/12/282 75/79 NS59/87, HMSO.

DES (1989d) *Planning for School Development. Report of the School Development Plans Project*, London, HMSO.

DES (1989e) *Local Education Authority Training Grants Scheme Financial Year 1990-91* — Circular 20/89 August 1989, HMSO.

DYER, C. (1988) 'Which Support'?: An examination of the term', *Support for Learning*, Vol. 3, No. 1, pp. 6–11.

EASEN, P. (1985) *Making School-Based INSET Work*, Open University/Croom Helm.

ELLIOTT, J. (1983) 'Action-Research: A framework for self-evaluation in schools', Working Paper No. 1, *Teacher-Pupil Interaction and the Quality of Learning Project*, Schools Council Programme 2, Cambridge Institute of Education.

ERAUT, M. (1984) 'Handling value issues', in ADELMAN, C. (Ed.) *The Politics and Ethics of Evaluation*, Croom Helm.

FULLAN, M. (1988) *What's Worth Fighting for in the Principalship?*, Toronto, Ontario Public School Teachers' Federation.

FULLER, F. (1969) 'Concerns of teachers: A developmental characterisation', *American Educational Research Journal*, **6**, pp. 207–26.

GASKILL, G. (1989) *The Advisory Teacher for Primary Science and Technology*, Association of Science Education.

GIPPS, C., CROSS, H. and GOLDSTEIN, H. (1987) *Warnock's Eighteen Percent: Children with Special Needs in Private Schools'*, Lewes, Falmer Press.

GRONN, P. C. (1983) 'Talk as the work: The accomplishment of school administration', *Administrative Science Quarterly*, **28**, pp. 1–21.

GIROUX, H. A. (1981) *Ideology, Culture and the Process of Schooling*, Chapter 2, Lewes, Falmer Press.

GOULD, S. and LETVEN, E. (1987) 'A center for interactive professional development', *Educational Leadership*, **45**, 3, pp. 49–52.

HAMMERSLEY, M. (1984) 'Staffroom news', in HARGREAVES, A. and WOODS, P. (Eds) *Classrooms and Staffrooms*, Milton Keynes, Open University Press.

HARGREAVES, D. (1982) *The Challenge of the Comprehensive School*, London, Routledge and Kegan Paul.

HEGARTY, S. (1988) 'Supporting the ordinary school', *British Journal of Special Education*, **15**, 2, pp. 50–3.

HERZBERG, F. (1966) 'Motivation — hygiene theory', in PUGH, D. (Ed.) *Organisation Theory*, Harmondsworth, Penguin.

HINSUN, M. (Ed.) (1987) *Teachers and Special Educational Needs*, Longman/NARE.

HOLLY, P., JAMES, T. and YOUNG, J. (1987) *The Experience of TRIST: Practitioners' Views of INSET and Recommendations for the Future* (DELTA PROJECT), M.S.C.

HOLLY, P. and SOUTHWORTH, G. (1989) *The Developing School*, Lewes, Falmer Press.

HOUSE OF COMMONS SELECT COMMITTEE (1986) *Achievement in Primary Schools*, Vol. 1, London, HMSO.

ILEA (1985) *Improving Primary Schools* (Report of the Committee on Primary Education) (The Thomas Report), London, ILEA.

JANE, E. and VARLAAM, A. (1981) 'Support for support teams', *INSIGHT*, **5**.1, Winter, pp. 29–31.

JEFFS, A. (1986) 'Motivation as a consideration in organisational change and staff development within a peripatetic support group', *Educational Management and Administration*, **14**, 1, pp. 39–48.

JONES, C. (1988) 'Advisory or support teachers in primary education?', *Education 3–13*, October, pp. 6–10.

JONES, G. (1969) *Planned Organisational Change*, London, Routledge and Kegan Paul.

JOYCE, B. and McKIBBIN, M. (1982) 'Teacher growth status and school environments', *Educational Leadership*, **40**, 2, pp. 36–41.

KEMMIS, S. (1980) 'Action Research in Retrospect', mimeo, presented at the Annual General Meeting of the Australian Association for Research in Education, Sydney, Australia (November 1980).

LAWTON, D. (1983) *Curriculum Studies and Educational Planning*, London, Hodder and Stoughton.

LEWIS, J. (1985) 'The theoretical underpinnings of school change strategies', in REYNOLDS, D. (Ed.) *Studying School Effectiveness*, Lewes, Falmer Press.

LIEBERMAN, A. (1986) 'Collaborative Research: Working with, not working on . . .', *Educational Leadership*, **43**, 5, pp. 28–31.

LIEBERMAN, A. (Ed.) (1988) *Building a Professional Culture in Schools*, New York, Teachers' College Press.

LITTLE, J.W. (1982) 'Norms of collegiality or experimentation: Workplace conditions of school success', *American Educational Research Journal*, **19**, 3, pp. 325–40.

LITTLE, J. W. (1988) 'Assessing the prospects for teacher leadership', in LIEBERMAN, A. (Ed.) *Building a Professional Culture in Schools*, New York, Teachers College Press.

LODGE, D. (1962) *Ginger you're Barmey*, MacGibbon and Kee.

LOFTHOUSE, B. (1987) 'Advisory teachers in primary education', *Education 3–13*, October, pp. 3–15.

LONG, S. (1988) 'Supporting teachers and children in topic work', in TANN, C. S. (Ed.) *Developing Topic Work in the Primary School*, Lewes, Falmer Press.

LORTIE, D. (1975) *School Teacher: A Sociological Study*, Chicago, University of Chicago Press.

MCLAUGHLIN, M. W. and YEE, S. M. (1988) 'School as a place to have a career', in LIEBERMAN, A. (Ed.) *Building a Professional Culture in Schools*, New York, Teachers' College Press.

MOSES, D., HEGERTY, S. and JOWETT, S. (1988) *Local Authority Support Services*, Windsor, NFER–Nelson.

NIAS, D.J. (1985) 'A more distant drummer: Teacher development as the development of self', in BARTON, L. and WALKER, S. (Eds) *Education and Social Change*, London, Croom Helm.

NIAS, D.J. (1987) 'Learning from difference: A collegial approach to change', in SMYTH, W.J. (Ed.) *Educating Teachers: Changing the Nature of Knowledge*, Lewes, Falmer Press.

NIAS, D.J. (1989) *Primary Teachers Talking: A Study of Teaching as Work*, London, Routledge.

NIAS, D.J., SOUTHWORTH, G. and YEOMANS, R. (1989) *Primary School Staff Relationships: A Study of School Culture*, London, Cassell.

PAQUETTE, M. (1987) 'Voluntary collegial support groups for teachers', in *Educational Leadership*, **45**, 3, pp. 36–9.

PENNINGTON, R. C. and GOODERHAM, D. G. (1987) 'Negotiation in School', Clyburn, Department Management Studies, Teesside Polytechnic.

PETRIE, P. (1988) 'Primary advisory teachers: Their value and their prospects', *Education 3–13*, October, pp. 3–5.

POLLARD, A. (1987) 'Primary school teachers and their colleagues', in DELAMONT, S. (Ed.) *The Primary School Teacher*, Lewes, Falmer Press.

REVANS, R. W. (1982) *Action Learning*, Chartwell Bratt.

RICHARDS, C. (1987) 'Primary education in England: An analysis of some recent issues and developments', in DELAMONT, S. (Ed.) *The Primary School Teacher*, Lewes, Falmer Press.

RISEBOROUGH, G. (1985) 'Pupils, teachers' careers and schooling: An empirical study', in BALL, B. and GOODSON, I. (Eds) *Teachers Lives and Careers*, Lewes, Falmer Press.

ROBINSON, G. S. (1990) 'RAMP — An Inservice Perspective', in AHMED, A. and WILLIAMS, H., *Raising Achievement in Mathematics Project 1986–89*, DES.

ROGERS, C. (1983) 'The challenge of present day teaching', *Freedom to Learn for the 80s*, Merrill, Columbus, Ohio.

SCHON, D. A. (1973) *Beyond the Stable State*, Pelican Books.

SCHON, D. A. (1983) *The Reflective Practitioner*, New York, Basic Books.

SILVER, H. (1987) *Education and the Research Process — Forming a New Republic?*, Council for National Academic Awards.

SMITH, C. J. and RICHMOND, R. C. (1988) 'Support for Special Needs — changing roles in an advisory service', *Educational Review*, **40**, 1, pp. 69–87.

SOULBURY COMMITTEE (1989) 'The Role and Function of Advisory Teachers'.

STENHOUSE, L. (1975) *An introduction to Curriculum Research and Development*, London, Heinemann.

STRAKER, N. (1988) 'Advisory teachers of mathematics: The ESG initiative', *Journal of Education Policy*, **3**, 4, pp. 371–84.

TUCKMAN, B. W. (1965) 'Development sequence in small groups', *Psychological Bulletin*, **63**, 6, pp. 384–99.

VANDERSLICE, G. (1983) *Communication for Empowerment*, New York, Cornell Univ. Media Services.

WEBB, R. (1989) 'Changing practice through consultancy-based INSET', *School Organisation*, **9**, 1, pp. 39–52.

WHYTE, W. F. (1955) *Street Corner Society*, University of Chicago Press, revised edition, first published 1943.

WILSON, L. (1987, 1988) Unpublished Fieldnotes.

WOODS, P. (1979) *The Divided School*, London, Routledge and Kegan Paul.

Index